ZEN
and the
MYSTIC IMPULSE

Reflections on the Teachings
of Willigis Jäger
Benedictine monk, mystic and Zen Master

by Arnie Lade

2025

First Edition: 2025

ISBN: 978-1-6086-9296-5

Library of Congress Control Number: 2025940543

On the Cover: "Golden Spiral" is a sculpture by Gisela Drescher that hangs in the meditation hall at Benediktushof, a Center for Meditation and Mindfulness in Germany. Gratefully used with the artist's permission.

Published by: **Lotus Press**
P.O. Box 325, Twin Lakes, WI 53181, USA
www.lotuspress.com | lotuspress@lotuspress.com
PH: (262) 889-8561

Dedicated to:

Willigis Jäger, OSB

(1925 - 2020)

©Björn Gaus

Table *of* Contents

Acknowledgements

I sincerely wish to express my gratitude to everyone who contributed to the success of this project. In particular, I thank the marvelous and generous team at Rivendell Retreat Center on Bowen Island, BC, for granting me three enriching extended writing retreats at the Penny Lou Cottage. I fondly remember those quiet, contemplative periods of solitude that laid the foundation for the thoughts and reflections that formed this book. What a beautiful place to contemplate the great mystery of life, surrounded by trees, ocean, and mountains!

I am deeply thankful to my friends and colleagues who played a crucial role in this project. I truly appreciate Terence Buie, Paulo de Costa, Judi Trost, Marie-André Horsthemke, Gisela Drescher, Christoph Quarch, and Franz-Nikolaus Müller for their unwavering advice, support, and encouragement. Their reviews of the manuscript at various stages and assistance with fine-tuning my German translations were invaluable. I also want to thank everyone at Benediktushof in Germany for their wholehearted assistance, as well as for continuing Willigis's mission and carrying his message forward.

I am immensely grateful to my wife, Diane, and my family for their steadfast support, which allowed me the time and space to bring this work to life. Lastly, I want to thank my friends and companions who share their spiritual journeys through everyday life. We are all connected—in gratitude, Gassho!

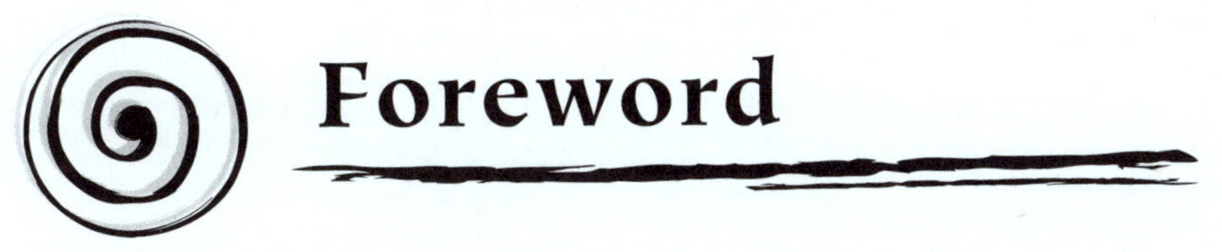

Foreword

As Arnie Lade recounts in his introduction, when being asked why he had made such a long journey to Benediktushof in Germany to study with Willigis Jäger, since there were so many teachers in North America, he answered: "Yes, it's true... but there is only one Willigis Jäger..." And this corresponds precisely to my own experience. Willigis Jäger was my most important teacher, for he was much more than just a *learned teacher* (Lesemeister); Willigis was a *master of spiritual life* (Lebensmeister) in the true sense, in accord with Meister Eckhart.

I first met Willigis Jäger more than 40 years ago and attended numerous courses with him over the years. I loved him as my most important teacher and, for many years, led contemplation courses with Willigis (as he preferred to be called).

For Willigis, Zen and contemplation, Buddhist and Christian paths, and beyond them, all the spiritual paths and practices of other great traditions were equal and authentic paths to the same goal. For this purpose, Willigis founded Benediktushof, an important *Center for Meditation and Mindfulness* today.

In *Zen and the Mystic Impulse*, the author, whom I have known for several years from Benediktushof, describes the essential aspects of Willigis' teachings. When I read the text, I remember with gratitude Willigis' many lectures and conversations with him that were ground-breaking for me and many others on the spiritual path.

Arnie has systematically and successfully formulated the principles of Willigis' teachings in ten chapters. He begins with the "mystical impulse" and continues through the following chapters, describing the spiritual and mystic path with its psychological implications and basic practices.

In the spirit of Willigis, the author draws on his rich experience with various spiritual traditions that have arisen from the fertile ground of the major world religions but which ultimately transcend their denominational boundaries to arrive at a common trans-confessional space, one that is known to the mystics.

Willigis often addressed the concept of a *philosophia perennis,* which recognizes a timeless, "eternal" wisdom in differing cultures and throughout the ages over the many thousands of years of humankind. In this context, the theological distinction between *cataphatic* and *apophatic*, which Willigis liked to address, is also helpful. Cataphatic means "following the word" and stands for the external side of the various religions with all their outward characteristics, from doctrine to rituals and practices to ethical principles. Meanwhile, apophatic refers to "away from the word," which refers to the internal side of religions or mystical core, which transcends the external confessional form. This mystical core is the origin and, ultimately, also the goal of religion. "The religions start from mysticism. There is no other way to start a religion," writes David Steindl-Rast.

This leads to the concept of a *theologia negativa*, which was fundamental to the development of Christian theology in the first centuries after Christ and his apostles and can also be found in differing forms in all major religions. Theologia negativa means that we can only ever say something provisional and incomplete about God, the divine, or whatever this highest, final reality is called and that words are used in the form of negation to express what God, the divine, is not; as well as to indicate that he/she/it is much more than words can express.

This brings to the fore the spiritual practice that Willigis and Arnie are concerned with, which involves recognizing who we really are, our purpose, and how to live accordingly. One of Willigis' favorite sayings has become particularly important to me: "We are not people who are having a spiritual experience, but spiritual beings who are having a human experience."

Franz Nikolaus Müller

Dr. Theology, Master in Philosophy and Psychology, Salzburg

Introduction

I had recently arrived at Benediktushof in Germany, and after our first dinner, those around the table introduced ourselves. When my turn came, I said I was from Canada's west coast. One curious and surprised person asked, "Why have you come to Germany from so far away when there are so many Zen teachers in North America?" I said, "Yes, that's true; there are many Zen teachers in North America, but there is only one Willigis Jäger, and he's here!"

I was inspired to travel to Germany in 2011 to study with a man I felt I must know—as if called by an inner force! Just a little over a year before, I had found one of his books in my local used book store; its title, *Search for the Meaning of Life: Essays and Reflections on the Mystical Experience,* had enticed me to take it from the shelf. The more I read, the more I couldn't put it down, for it seemed to speak directly to me.

After reading my first book by Willigis Jäger, I tracked down another of his English-translated books, which I devoured with equal enthusiasm. It, too, was significant. Gradually, the wish arose in me to study with him, and as often happens with what seems inevitable, life conspired to bring me to his teaching center in Holzkirchen, a small village in northern Bavaria, the following summer. Once there, I was surprised to meet a man who wore no robe or title; everybody referred to him as Willigis. He was most welcoming, with a respectful, approachable, and grounded demeanor. I can genuinely say that my life has changed dramatically since encountering him as a person and, before that, through his writings. That year, Willigis became my Zen teacher.

This book is a tapestry of many spiritual threads - of mystical teachings and traditions, especially Zen and Contemplation. It is also about how and why we enter the mystical journey. I write from personal experiences and my understanding gained through life and practice. I write about my teacher, Willigis Jäger, a Benedictine monk, priest, and Zen Master, and what he taught. I also share many engaging quotes and poems by other writers and teachers that speak to the book's various spiritual and mystical themes.

Willigis was one of Europe's most influential Zen and Christian contemplation teachers and founded one of the continent's largest retreat and teaching centers. He was a unique Zen Master recognized and confirmed in both the Japanese Zen and Chinese Chan traditions; his formal Zen name and title was Koun Rōshi. Willigis accompanied thousands of students on their spiritual journey, mainly from German-speaking lands, while others, like myself, came from far and wide. He wrote over 20 books on Zen, Christian contemplation, and spirituality in German, some of which are national bestsellers. Many of his books were translated into other languages, but unfortunately, all his English-language books are now out of print. He was never well known in North America, except for a few of us who had the privilege of knowing and studying with him. In part, this book is my attempt to bring forth his essential teachings and vision of spirituality to readers who may never otherwise encounter one of the great spiritual teachers of our times. I have included a short biographical sketch of Willigis's life in the Appendix if you wish to learn about his journey and what informed his teachings.

Mysticism is the path of transformation that leads to fulfillment, renewed meaning, and becoming an authentic, whole person. This journey is brought about through rediscovery and connection to the ground of one's being and through finding true belonging in life to something greater than oneself.

I intend to give an overview of this mystical path - including the search for meaning and belonging, the role of prayer and meditation, living in the present moment, finding precepts to live by, the value of teachers and mentors, reflections on death and dying, and much more. I cover the significant themes that Willigis talked about and wrote about in his life with direct quotes from his writings. I share my reflections on these topics and what has helped me on my journey of spiritual practice.

This book does not focus on specific practice techniques per se, a subject best left for individual instruction by a teacher. And, if you already have an established practice and spiritual path, this book will broaden your horizons.

This book was conceived after Willigis passed away in 2020. His death was just before humanity became paralyzed by the arrival of the COVID-19 virus. Around the same time, within days of each other, my older brother, Alfred, had also died. My world was upside down for a while - with two significant persons in my life dying, plus the new reality of COVID and the shutting down of everyday life and the scrambling to survive the unknown, as well as my wife and I being in the middle of a significant work move. I didn't seem to have much time to process any of it. But slowly, as the months went by and life started to return to a new routine, there began to be time to integrate all the loss and changes.

As I reflected on Willigis and his impact on my life, I felt a strong desire to honor him. Over the course of several months, the idea gradually developed to write about my experiences, highlighting the wonderful teachings and inspiration I received from him and his writings. This book is my testimony to what I learned from Willigis and what is spiritually alive in me today.

Looking back, I can recall Willigis suggesting that I write more. The first time was after I had given him a couple of my books on healing as a token of appreciation. Those books had been translated into German, and I thought he'd be interested in their content. He talked to me a few days later, thanked me, and encouraged me to keep writing. At the time, I told Willigis I didn't feel I had anything more to write about. He left it at that. But Willigis was persistent and, some say, highly intuitive; a year later, he casually told me again that I should write more. I never did until now, but I hope I have done justice to his persistence, for this is my gift in honor of Willigis's legacy.

Unlike many of his students and followers, I only spent a relatively short time with Willigis when he was already in his elder years. What is most important, though, is what was transmitted and received; this book is my humble attempt to express just that. On a personal level, there was always great warmth and caring in our interactions, as there was mutuality and a natural bond. I fondly remember him giving me his loving blessings and well-wishes each time I departed from Germany to return home.

Most importantly, in Willigis's teachings, I found a spiritual home. There wasn't much resistance in me to his teachings but rather a sense of agreement with what I already felt to be true. There was also an emotional and spiritual healing in being with Willigis, which I now recognize as having to do with my Catholic upbringing and Germanic origins. I was born in Germany, and my family immigrated to Canada when I was three. But we never discussed this; my healing happened on its own accord through being with Willigis. On reflection, it was a time of spiritual quickening, apparently, one that I was ready for.

Willigis was a kindred spirit. He transmitted something beyond words, which I felt in his presence. Even now, when I close my eyes and tune in, I have a felt sense of his presence and innate stillness. During the first week of training that I attended with Willigis, I was given a seat next to him in the meditation hall at Benediktushof. I meditated beside Willigis for many hours each day; his inner stillness and quiet had set me at ease and allowed me to sink into being present in meditation and to all the surrounding unfamiliarity of the place. That feeling of his presence is still alive in me today and a reminder that there's still only one Willigis—right here, now, in the stillness.

CHAPTER 1

The Mystic Impulse

I

In the depth of my being, there has always been a sense, a knowing, that there is something *More,* a *Presence*, something much greater than myself to which I am intimately connected. You might call that *More* or *Presence* by a different holy name - maybe you'd say: God, Creator, Brahman, Abba, the Eternal, Tao, Great Spirit, Buddha Nature, the Unborn, Allah, or perhaps some other word. Then again, for you, maybe there's no name for this *Presence*—only an intuition, a felt sense of something greater, in which you are part and parcel of.

People and religions have historically used words, images, and ideas to point to a fundamental and transcendent spiritual reality. Yet this very telling is in Zen said to be like a finger pointing to the moon, warning us to be mindful not to mistake the finger for the moon. The transcendent cannot be grasped and boxed in by words formed by ideas within the intellect. As the Chinese sage Lao Tsu says, "The Tao that can be told is not the eternal Tao; the name that can be named is not the eternal name."[1]

And still, we try to express, just as I am doing here in this writing, something that is inexpressible. As conscious beings, we continually try to point to the moon through poetic words, sacred gestures, art, dance, and song to give transparency to these profound spiritual experiences and understanding. And in hopes of sharing its discovery and love with others.

Willigis Jäger often referred to a first reality and common timeless source of human spiritual experience, which he called the *sophia perennis,* or eternal wisdom, a wellspring from which all genuine spiritual teachings arose, unbound from belief or creed. He writes: "Sophia perennis is not a

1. Gui-fu Feng & Jane English *Tao Te Ching by Lao Tsu* (New York: Vintage Books, 1989), 3.

religion. Rather, it is a dimension wherein we are gifted with the experience of the true Self. It is the essence of all religions, an encounter with a reality from which all religions arise and towards which all religions strive."[2]

Many years before, in India, my revered teacher, Sri Haidakhan Babaji (d.1984), referred to this spiritual source as *Sanatana dharma,* which he described as "the eternal, universal law without beginning or end. No one knows when it came into being or how long it will exist. At the beginning of Creation, it was the only religion, and at the end of Creation, it will be the only religion. Sanatana dharma is like an ocean into which all other dharmas, like rivers, merge."[3]

Indeed, many great mystics, philosophers, and spiritual teachers have spoken about a primal reality or experience, one that precedes words, concepts, and images. These mystics and teachers tell us that this first reality is a truth that will always exist, even though we may not apprehend it. They also tell us that this truth, this eternal source, can be experienced within us.

The renowned 16th-century Spanish mystic, John of the Cross, in his *Spiritual Canticle*, writes poetically about this eternal wellspring:

That eternal spring is hidden, for I know well where it has
its rise, although it is night.
I do not know its origin, nor has it one, but I know that
every origin has come from it, although it is night. [4]

Swami Vivekananda, the influential early 20th-century Indian teacher who brought the teachings of Vedanta from India to the West, likened this spiritual principle of an eternal source to gravity, an ever-present

2. Willigis Jäger *Timeless Eternal Wisdom* translated by Marie-André Horsthemke (Dublin: Logos Publications, 2014), 9. & also Willigis Jäger *Wiederkehr der Mystik* (Freiburg im Breisgau: Herder Verlag, 2004), 154-156.

3. Radhe Shyam *I Am Harmony* (Crestone, CO: Spanish Creek Publishing, 1990) 109. & Pritam Rajshi *The Gospel of Babaji (*Edmonton: Roche Miette Books, 2024), 125.

4. Willigis Jäger *Wiederkehr der Mystik* (Freiburg im Breisgau: Herder Verlag, 2004), 107. & for reference, see Kieran Kavanaugh & Otilio Rodriguez *The Collected Works of St. John of the Cross.* (Washington: ICS Publications, 1991), 58-59.

intrinsic reality here on Earth. Yet, as individuals or species, we have not always perceived gravity, its nature, or its existence.

Aldous Huxley (1894-1963), the writer and philosopher, called this first reality the *perennial philosophy* as witnessed in the world's mystic traditions. His many writings on the subject are a masterful and comprehensive articulation of the underlying unity of the human experience in this mystical and spiritual reality. I believe, in particular, Huxley's book *The Perennial Philosophy* is an important thesis that underlies what mystics like Willigis point towards.[5] I am also glad to have read Huxley's book before encountering Willigis's writing, for they mutually affirmed my conviction of the universality of the human spiritual experience and inspired me to study with Willigis in Germany.

Huxley gives a basic outline of the perennial philosophy in his essay The Minimum Working Hypothesis. This essay appeared in the book *Vedanta for the Western World,*[6] and what follows is my paraphrasing of Huxley's insights:

- There is an unmanifested principle of all manifestations, known as Godhead, Ground, Brahman, Unborn, Eternal, and so forth.
- That it is possible for human beings to know, love, and become one with the divine Eternal.
- Reaching this realization and awareness is the purpose of human existence.
- That there is a Dharma (or virtuous path) that must be obeyed and a Tao (or way) that must be followed if humans are to achieve this goal.

5. Aldous Huxley *The Perennial Philosophy* (New York: Harper Collins, 1945)
6. Christopher Isherwood, editor *Vedanta for the Western World* (London: Allen & Unwin, 1948), 34.

¤ And, the more there is of the self, the less there is of the Eternal. Therefore, the Tao is the way of humility and love, and Dharma is a living principle of relinquishing selfishness and pursuing self-transcending awareness.

II

Willigis often said that all true spiritual paths lead to the same summit despite their different approaches. This summit is transpersonal, where we step past our limited self-identification and belief structures to recognize our living relationship to the source or ground of our being. It is a breakthrough to a new way of being, marked by deepening love and compassion for others and our world. This new awareness says YES to one's life—here and now—and all that life entails!

As one walks the mystic's path, love and humility unfold and blossom in one's heart. This love is born from recognizing that the very ground of being, indeed of all things in this creation, is rooted in an incomprehensible love. And so, my task is to live out of this love as best as possible.

As we walk this path, we recognize that one of our most profound yearnings is for true belonging. A yearning that is only truly satisfied when we experience our true nature, a spiritual homecoming. And if and when we do, we resolve the fundamental questions of our existence, such as why we suffer, are born, and must die. For many, these questions call them to lead a spiritual life. Also, feelings of self-isolation, dissatisfaction and meaninglessness, the nature of evil, and the mystery of life can motivate us to search for the Eternal.

And when we're no longer satisfied by the spiritual answers prescribed in books or by teachers, we might just be ready to be touched by the mystic impulse, the desire to drink from the fountain of experience. The first time I attended a training retreat with Willigis, I asked him to sign one of his books for me; he wrote: *Those who drink from the source need not drink from the bottle.* We take up this quest when we become willing to become teachable, open, and transparent to transcendency, something greater than our limited self.

In Zen, this spiritual quest is called taking up the *Great Matter* of birth and death. This journey leads through the encounter of our most profound personal koans or questions at the crucible of all the paradoxes and dilemmas in one's life, the ones that cannot be answered rationally. As Willigis once told me in response to a deep, personal problem that I was working through, "Most questions are unanswerable, at least the important ones!" The answers lie in a transcendent experience—an experience that emerges spontaneously, that, by nature, is beyond the conditioned, rational self, out of which new perspectives and meanings emerge. In doing so, we can come to terms with life as it has been given to us in this existence, this place, and time.

III

One of Willigis's frequently used analogies in describing the varieties of spiritual and religious experience throughout human history is that of light shining through stained glass, such as in a church. The pure sunlight diffuses and, at the same time, is tinted and tainted by the various colors, images, and forms through the glass. Similarly, in mystical experiences, the individual expresses the one transcendent light (or reality) through their lived experience using words, images, songs, and other unique intimations of their personality and conditioning. This conveys the inexpressible joy of breaking through into a whole new awareness.

As mentioned, the mystical experience is beyond the horizon of understanding, limited by the ego and rational mind. This limited self is invariably dualist and cannot know or perceive itself directly. The gateway that bridges this duality and leads to transcendent unity is an awakening, which, in Zen, is referred to as *seeing one's (true) nature* (kenshō in Japanese). The great mystics of all traditions can only give us images, metaphors, and analogies to convey this experience.

Willigis said that the urge and challenge of trying to express the mystical experience is like that of a lover who wishes to express their affection through poetry or song. Mystics often use vivid imagery to convey the richness of their encounters with the transcendent; for example, the Dominican mystic Johannes Tauler wrote: "The mind probes the depths of the absolute to the point that it loses any sense of differentiation. It becomes so unified with the divine that it permeates one's entire being. Just as a drop of water loses itself in a vat of wine, the mind dissolves, eliminating distinctions and creating a mysterious stillness and undifferentiated oneness." We must appreciate that mystical language attempts to express an all-encompassing oneness that arises from the indescribable depths of the absolute. John of the Cross beautifully captures the difficulty of describing the indescribable when he wrote: "I entered in I knew not where and stayed there without knowing, transcending all knowledge. I knew nothing of the place I had entered."[7]

The touching of this first reality that is beyond words and images, beyond duality, leads invariably to an opening of the heart wherein love and compassion flow, wherein true intimacy with life is felt—a homecoming to life's fullness. The mystic knows there is no withdrawing from life but only participation in the mystery of life. John of the Cross, while being imprisoned and persecuted, expresses his divine love for God in the very intimacy of life with these words:

My Beloved is the mountains,
The solitary wooded valleys,
The strange islands,
The roaring torrents,
The whisper of the amorous gales;
The tranquil night, at the approach of dawn,
The silent music,
The murmuring solitude,
The supper which revives,
and enkindles love. [8]

This intimacy with nature and seeing the transcendent in all things reminds me of all the beautiful Zen and Taoist poetry of the East, which I have enjoyed most of my life. One of my favorites is the following poem by an unknown author I once found many years ago during my travels in China. This poem is undated but harkens to Zen's formative period, which Taoism greatly influenced.

When the wild birds sing their melodies
from the treetops,
they carry the voices of the Ancestors.
When the mountain flowers bloom,
their fragrance carries the true meaning of the Tao. [9]

To the mystic, God is not out there, somewhere beyond creation, but right here and now, in and around us, when the illusion of separateness is dropped. In the Buddhist tradition, the Heart Sutra chanted daily in many temples says there is no difference between form and emptiness. The word form connotes all of reality, while emptiness is another name for what the Buddha called the Unborn. His awakening under the Bodhi tree led him to live a life of great compassion and engagement by helping others.

In reading mystical writings, we must be mindful of the limitation of words and images and the seemingly innate urge to try to understand the unknowable by thinking. For the very nature of ordinary consciousness is, as Zen scriptures warn: "like a sword that cuts, but cannot cut itself; like an eye that sees, but cannot see itself."[10] Rather, it is more helpful to let the words and images of sacred writings be read like suggestive poetry or seen like art that conveys a felt sense that intimates and points us to the sacred.

7. Willigis Jäger *Ewige Weisheit* (München: Kösel-Verlag, 2011), 75-76.

8. Willigis Jäger *My Beloved is the Mountains* (Congers, NY: Cistercian Studies Quarterly, 1984, article in Volume 19.3) 255-266. & Otilio Rodriguez *The Collected Works of St. John of the Cross.* (Washington: ICS Publications, 1991), 76.

9. For a different version of this poem, see Chuang Chung-yuan: *Creativity and Taoism - A Study of Chinese Philosophy, Art and Poetry* (New York Harper Colophon, 1963), 113.

10. Alan Watts with Al Chung-Liang Huang *The Watercourse Way* (New York: Pantheon Books, 1975), 49.

The 14th-century Zen Master Dai-o Kokushi advises, "There is a reality before heaven and earth. Indeed, it has no form, much less a name. Eyes fail to see it; it has no voice for ears to detect... O, my good friends gathered here if you desire to listen to the thunderous voice of the Dharma, exhaust your words, empty your thoughts, for then you may come to recognize this one Essence."[11]

IV

Mysticism is all too frequently misunderstood and confused with lofty, ecstatic states and paranormal experiences such as clairvoyance, precognition, rapture, and visions. In authentic mysticism, such parapsychic phenomena may occur, but they are viewed more as obstacles and distractions that can lead one astray. The aim is not some self-centered, detached ecstasy but the recognition and union with the Eternal and becoming a whole person, thereby fulfilling one's humanity. More simply, mysticism looks into the mystery of being alive in this unimaginable universe and its meaning.

Mystics are ordinary people who can be found inside and outside formal religions. They include people who profess indigenous spirituality or follow more than one spiritual tradition and even those who consider themselves agnostic or atheist. I have met such folks in many Zen retreats, yet they are profoundly mystical and committed to their practice, for mysticism goes beyond religious and spiritual identification.

Brother David Steindl-Rast (1926-), a fellow Benedictine monk, noted author, and friend of Willigis, writes: "We do a great disservice to mystics by putting them on a pedestal and thinking of them as a special kind of human being. The truth is that every human being is a special kind of mystic, and that creates a tremendous challenge for each one of us to become precisely the mystic we are meant to be. Here, I'm taking mysticism in the strictest sense as the experience of communion with Ultimate Reality. All of us are certainly called to experience this

11. Daisetz Teitaro Suzuki *Manual of Zen Buddhism* (London: Rider and Co., 1950), 145-146.

communion. And there's no one and never will be anyone and never has been anyone who can experience Ultimate Reality in the same way in which you can experience it. Therefore, you are called to be that special kind of mystic that only you can be."[12]

The early 20th-century Sufi mystic Hazrat Inayat Khan writes: "No one can be a mystic and call himself a Christian mystic, a Jewish mystic or a Mohammedan mystic. For what is mysticism? Mysticism is something which erases from one's mind all idea of separateness, and if a person claims to be this mystic or that mystic, he is not a mystic; he is only playing with a name." Also, "There is one God and one truth, one religion and one mysticism; call it Sufism or Christianity or Hinduism or Buddhism, or whatever you wish. As God cannot be divided, so mysticism cannot be divided. It is an error when someone says, 'My religion is different from yours.' He does not know what religion means. Neither can there be many mysticisms, just as there cannot be many wisdoms; there is one wisdom."[13]

The great 13th-century Sufi master Muhyi al-Din Ibn al-Arabi expresses this same sentiment when he writes: "If the believer understood the meaning of the saying 'the color of the water is the color of the receptacle,' he would admit the validity of all beliefs, and he would recognize God in every form and every object of faith."[14]

David Steindl-Rast echoes the universal nature of mysticism in *The Way of Silence;* he writes: "The Mystery is not limited to Christianity. It belongs to basic human spirituality. We encounter Mystery as the 'Nothing' from which everything comes. The origin of everything at every moment is a leap from Nothing into Being. The mystery is the source of Being."[15]

Mystics of all faiths teach that our encounter with this great Mystery goes far beyond what can be said and is open to us all, irrespective of

12. David Steindl-Rast *The Way of Silence* (Cincinnati: Franciscan Media, 2016), 39.
13. Hazrat Inayat Khan *The Sufi Message Vol. X - Sufi Mysticism* (Delhi: Motilal Banarsidass, 1990), 24 & 27.
14. Muhyi al-Din Ibn al-Arabi *Fusus al-hikam* Internet source: https://ibnarabisociety.org/introduction-muhyiddin-ibn-arabi/
15. David Steindl-Rast *i am through you so i* (New York: Paulist Press, 2017), 85-86.

belief. And this Mystery is not different from the very ground of being within us.

V

Yet, all too often in the narratives of established religions, the metaphors depicted in their sacred writings, symbols, and images can act to block us from their spiritual meaning. This occurs when we get stuck in their literal or rational interpretation if and when we start from the premise that metaphors are facts. For example, how do we reconcile modern science's understanding of reality with the notion of Heaven and Hell as physical destinations? How shall we interpret the biblical story of Jesus rising from the dead and ascending into Heaven or Elijah going up into Heaven in his chariot? What meaning do we give Heaven in the twenty-first century when our scientific understanding paints a picture of the unimaginable universe of vast, seemingly unbounded magnitude? The scriptural metaphors in the classic holy books only make sense from a spiritual interpretation and mythological perspective; otherwise, they quickly become viewed as meaningless and relegated to fiction.

This is why the mystics tell us that God, the Eternal, ultimate reality, transcends all delineation of categories and concepts, such as object and subject, noun and verb.

As Joseph Campbell (1904-1987), the famous American mythologist, pointed out, one of the essential functions of sacred myths is to help us realize the mystical dimension behind the surface phenomenology of the world. And that this transcendent mystery source is also within ourselves. Campbell also observed that the concept of God as a personality can hinder our search, and breaking past this notion is necessary to embrace the transpersonal, mystical dimension. He wrote: "This [notion] is so drummed into us that the word 'God' refers to a personality. Now, there have been very important mystics who have broken past that. For instance, Meister Eckhart, whose line I'd like to quote is 'the ultimate leave-taking is the leaving of God for God.'"[16]

Indeed, in my life, I had once felt hampered by my concepts of God and religious teachings. I was raised and taught in the Roman Catholic tradition at home and school. Bible stories had a certain appeal when I was young; they touched a sense of wonder, mystery, and yearning in me. But at a certain age, there was a disconnect between the stories, images, and teachings of the Church compared to my maturing awareness of life around me and my negative experiences within my Catholic school. Sadly, no one instructed me on how to read these stories and see the religious symbols in a more profound, more meaningful way, one that could inspire me to continue growing in my spiritual formation. Over time, I became increasingly disengaged from my religion and its teachings, which seemed so separate from the reality around me growing up that I began to doubt their meaningfulness.

This doubt fully blossomed during my teen years, especially after a personal experience in which I experienced an out-of-body, near-death-like state—an experience that deeply affected me. On reflection, I now recognize this experience as transpersonal and spiritual, which awakened my mystic impulse and desire to settle the Great Matter, to use the Zen saying. After that, I kept seeing things as quite different from what I had been taught, and eventually, my doubts trumped my beliefs, and I left the church.

Only later in life, when I met Willigis, was I able to heal my relationship with my religious upbringing. I had finally found the mystical tradition in Christianity that spoke to me, one that honored all sacred paths, some of which I had journeyed along before meeting Willigis.

Today, the Christian and all the world's holy writings, religious images, symbols, and sacred places are sources of inspiration and affirmation for me. Their songs, poems, stories, and prayers can open my heart and connect me to the divine. The mystic path teaches us that there is only one essential journey to our true nature, which is none other than total love. And, as I mature spiritually, I endeavor to remain open to all authentic

16. Joseph Campbell in Conversation with Michael Toms *An Open Life* (New York: Larson Publications, 1988), 55.

spiritual traditions and, at the same time, to the transformation of all my beliefs, images, and concepts that hold me back from experiencing the divine!

The following is one of Ibn al-Arabi's most elegant and well-known poems, in which he declares the way of Love, as seen in all its religious forms:

O Marvel, a garden among the flames!

My heart has grown capable of taking
any form:
a pasture for gazelles,
an abbey for Christian monks,

a temple for idols,
Kaaba for the circling pilgrim,
the tables of the Torah,
the scrolls of the Qur'ān.

I follow the religion of Love

whatever way Love's caravan takes,
that shall be my religion and faith. [17]

17. Muhyi al-Din Ibn al-Arabi *Poem 11 - Tarjuman Al-Ashfaq* Internet source: https://ibnarabisociety.org/poetry-poems & for the German translation: Willigis Jäger Über Die Liebe (München: Kösel-Verlag, 2011), 50.

CHAPTER 2

Coming Out of the Ego Tunnel

I

The first time I came to Willigis's center in Holzkirchen for summer training, I was deeply moved and inspired by the readings and recitations used during the daily schedule. The writings were drawn from the world's spiritual teachings, especially Zen and Christian contemplative literature. The words of the 14th-century Christian mystic Johannes Tauler seemed to speak to me directly, especially the following verse:

Let your images of things go completely,
and keep your Temple empty.
For when the Temple is empty
and the fantasies are put away,
then you will be a house of God and not before.
You will no longer be disturbed by that
which has given you grief and suffering. [1]

Christian mystics, like Tauler, often used the metaphor of letting go and emptying in their teachings, just as Hindu and Buddhist scriptures use the metaphor of detaching and releasing. During that first retreat with Willigis, I found there was much to let go of and release. I sometimes spontaneously wept in meditation without any attached cognitive story behind the emotions. However, there was a tremendous feeling of relief and joy, a deep sense of homecoming with Willigis and being at Benediktushof.

1. P. Ermin Döll *Der Weg der Meister* (Dietfurt/Altmühltal: Meditationhaus St. Frazsiskus, 2005), 86. & see also Willigis Jäger & Beatrice Grimm *Die Flötedes Unendlichen* (Holzkirchen, DE: Wege-Der-Mystik, 2009), 44. Translated by Arnie Lade.

In the last chapter, I used the word transcending frequently, which is what happens when we do let go spiritually. However, what do we transcend on the journey towards the ground of being, our true nature? Simply put, we transcend, let go of, empty, or detach from our narrow, self-centered ego, often called the small self. Transcendence does not mean getting rid of the ego or becoming a non-person; instead, it means bringing the ego into a new relationship within ourselves. Many great mystics and spiritual teachers often had strong personalities. This was true of Willigis, too; I found him warm, intuitive, nonjudgemental, purposeful, and energetic, with natural charisma and eloquence.

Willigis wrote: "In Mysticism, we realize that the ego is just as much a manifestation of the original reality as anything else. But because it experiences itself as a reality above others, the ego is not less me but more me." Again, "Mysticism doesn't want to conquer the ego or fight with it. It simply wants to show the ego its limits, to give it the importance it deserves, yet not more. Thus, mysticism attempts to see the ego for what it is: an organizational center for the personality structure of the individual."[2]

When the ego is brought into the right relationship with the ground of being, a widening capacity for love and connection with humanity and the world occurs. In time, when walking the mystic's path, the ego's illusion of separateness diminishes, and a more spacious sense of wholeness emerges. But we do not lose the ego, the little self; instead, a new way of living emerges from being in touch with our true nature.

II

In listening to Willigis's talks during that first retreat, he often used a curious word, the *ego tunnel,* when talking about this self-centered part of us. He once said: "The question being hotly debated today is: what is our ego? Can consciousness be traced back to neurological states? In

2. Willigis Jäger *Mysticism for Modern* Times translated by Christoph Quarch (Liguori, Missouri: Liguori-Triumph, 2006), 5-6.

3. Thomas Metzinger *The Ego Tunnel* (New York: Basic Books, 2009).

other words, does our brain produce consciousness, or is it just a receiver or instrument? Our ego has no continuity. Thomas Metzinger calls it the *ego tunnel* in his book.[3] Our job is to come out of the ego tunnel as awake people.... we can then realize that our true being is much more comprehensive and enduring than this superficial me. This *me* will die, but our true nature will live on, materialized in a new form."[4]

Metzinger and Willigis say that the ego is fundamentally tunnel-visioned, giving each of us our unique experience of reality. We do not experience the *real* world unfiltered, for we perceive reality through individual conditioning and interpretation. The sciences teach us that we cannot know the breadth and depth of reality at any given moment; it is not in our nervous system's capacity to do so. Our human nervous system is only configured to take in a limited amount of information via the sense faculties; for example, we can perceive only a small range of light and sound within their full spectrum. And what's taken in through the senses is further honed and filtered by our brain before it reaches our conscious perception.

The same is true with our thinking; we are usually only aware of the surface layer of thoughts and not the depths of consciousness while awake or sleeping. Instead, we inhabit a uniquely filtered mind and body consciousness formed and informed by all the prior causes and conditions in one's life. Out of which arises a feeling, a notion of "I"—of self-identity and self-apartness. Meanwhile, our thinking, emotions, perceptions, and beliefs continually inform, confirm, and modify our sense of "I" ness.

David Bohm, the 20th-century physicist and philosopher, said in a 1977 lecture in Berkeley: "Reality is what we take to be true. What we take to be true is what we believe. What we believe is based upon our perceptions. What we perceive depends on what we look for. What we look for depends on what we think. What we think depends on what we perceive. What we perceive determines what we believe. What we

4. Erhard Meyer-*Leben im Goldenen Wind* (Berlin: Frieling-Verlag, 2011), 75.

believe determines what we take to be true. What we take to be true is our reality."[5]

The American Zen teacher Joko Beck (1917-2011) put it starkly when she said: "It isn't real or unreal; it is just what it is. But opinions, judgments, memories, dreaming about the future—ninety percent of thoughts spinning around in our heads have no essential reality. And we go from birth to death, unless we wake up, wasting most of our life with them."[6]

III

Inherent in the human ego structure is the problem of implicit duality in how we perceive ourselves, our autonomy and separateness, and the life around us. It also gave rise to our sense of uniqueness, superiority, and arrogance. Since the earliest times, humans have been grappling to explain the origins of this sense of duality and separateness through stories, images, and myths. The Bible gives us the myth of the fall of man in the Garden of Eden when the first people, Adam and Eve, disobeyed God's instructions and ate from the fruit of the Knowledge of Good and Evil. Afterward, the story goes, they were exiled from God's timeless presence in paradise and became aware of themselves as naked with self-awareness and shame.

In other religions and cultures, different myths, images, and stories explain the human awareness of an underlying duality. For example, Swami Venkatesananda (1921-1982), in his talks on the classic Hindu text *Patanjali's Yoga Sutras*, describes duality arising in the following scheme: out of Supreme Unity arose Cosmic Intelligence and Cosmic Ignorance. And, out of this same taint of Ignorance within us comes the idea of "I" or ego-sense, and once the concept of "I" is there, it becomes the center of everything. From this, "I" duality arises, on the one hand,

5. Mattieu Ricard & Trinh Xuan Thuan *Quantum and the Lotus* (New York: Crown Publishers, 2001), 121.
6. Joko Beck *Everyday Zen*. (San Francisco: HarperOne, 1989), 7.

attraction, approval, or liking, and on the other hand, repulsion, rejection, or dislike.[7]

A similar motif is also found in the Buddhist teachings of the three unwholesome roots or poisons: greed, anger, and delusion (sometimes called clinging, aversion, and ignorance). The suffering of the three poisons separates us from our true essence, while the wholesome antidotes of generosity, loving-kindness, and wisdom liberate and allow us to reconnect with our Buddha nature.

From this ego-sense of "I" identification, awareness of duality arises in its many forms: right and wrong, Creator and Creation, enlightenment and ignorance, Nirvana and Samsara, you and me, man and woman, love and hate, liking and disliking, friend and enemy, right and left, time and space, aversion and clinging, and so on.

When we connect to our deepest selves, we can transcend the confines of the ego tunnel, and thus, suffering diminishes, and a new awareness emerges—one that is more alive to the present moment. We become worthy of our highest calling: a noble love and compassion for each other and all of life. The noted American psychologist Abraham Maslow puts transcendence at the apex of human needs. of which he says: "Transcendence refers to the very highest and most inclusive or holistic levels of human consciousness, behaving and relating, as ends rather than means, to oneself, to significant other, to human beings in general, to other species, to nature, and to the cosmos."[8]

Willigis once remarked that we have become so disconnected from others and the world around us that it's as if we have been penalized by an ego that isolates us. He said that our ego structure inevitably creates fences and barriers between us, causing us to claim ownership of things, defend what we have, or try to acquire from others. We've lost sight of the fact that we are not truly separate from one another and that we have

7. Swami Venkatesanada *The I-dea of I* (Cape Province, South Africa: Chiltern Yoga Trust, 1973), 34-36.
8. Abraham Maslow *Various Meaning of Transcendence* (Journal of Transpersonal Psychology 1969), 66.

to break free from the self-limiting vision of our ego to experience our unity and oneness with all.[9]

The tragedy is that we, as a species, are trapped within a collective ego tunnel. Today, the very survival of the human species and countless life forms on this precious earth depends upon a transformation of our human-centric narcissism. Ecological disasters, the continuing wars, and the possibility of nuclear annihilation threaten the whole planet. We urgently need to move past this stage of human evolution, where the ego dominates human thinking and actions. Individually and collectively, there is an urgent necessity for a conscious shift of perspective from the personal to the transpersonal, from human-focused to earth-centered. The path of transformation from the ego tunnel is the road all mystics and great spiritual teachers have taken. This road is wide open for anyone to walk, irrespective of belief, culture, or position.

IV

Innumerable emotional afflictions arise from the ego's sense of separateness, such as feelings of alienation, loneliness, despair, unloveableness, guilt, and shame. All these afflictions amplify this feeling that we are apart from the world we live in, not a part of. When we can go beyond ourselves, our limited egoic, little self, we become ready for a rebirth into a spiritual life. Often, great emotional distress, isolation, the anguish of a meaningless life, or the fear of death can lead us to search for inner transformation and something greater than ourselves, if we persist. Such great suffering can crack the barrier of the little self and make us permeable to our ground of being and the transcendent.

I believe, as Willigis did, that the spiritual challenge of our times is to balance the ego structure so that it becomes less dominant and tunnel-visioned. This will allow us to widen our capacity for compassion for

9. Willigis Jäger *Ewige Weisheit* (München: Kösel-Verlag, 2011), 78.

10. P. Ermin Döll *Der Weg der Meister* (Dietfurt/Altmühltal: Meditationhaus St. Frazsiskus, 2005), 243. & see also Willigis Jäger & Beatrice Grimm *Die Flötedes Unendlichen* (Holzkirchen, DE: Wege-Der-Mystik, 2009), 44. Translated & adapted by Arnie Lade.

ourselves and others. As the 20th-century Indian teacher Sri Nisargadatta once said, *the mind creates the abyss; the heart crosses it.*

In my own life, I know that there is a place within me that is uncluttered and spacious and connects me to unconditional love and benevolence (agape). It is a still place that reveals itself when I put down my images, thoughts, and fantasies; it's a place of unknowing and the cauldron of transformation that ripens and widens my heart. I intend to keep practicing to embody this awareness, and I know from experience that suffering arises when I forget my connection – it's no easy task, but an essential one. For me, the mystical path lies in Zen, contemplative, and awareness practices. Mine has not been a smooth or perfect journey, but the growing capacity of love heartens me. It's about progress, not perfection!

The Dominican mystic Johannes Tauler encourages us to let go of the limited, small self that clings to desires, ideas, and possessions. We start to let go when we train ourselves to abide in awareness, which is at the heart of meditation and mindfulness practices, so that suffering from our self-centeredness diminishes. Tauler said:

When one abides with inner awareness,
the "I" loses hold.

That "I" that wanted to have things,
that knew things,
that wished for things.

Until this clinging to things perish,
one faces suffering.

This does not happen in one day,
nor in a short time.

By letting go, humility and diligence
inner awareness grows.

And with time and perseverance,
this will become easy and satisfying.[10]

CHAPTER 3

Unity, Belonging and Transcendence

I

For me, God, the Eternal, the Unborn is not distant—but a living presence within and around me, in which the natural world is a revelation of the Eternal's majesty. I often find solace in nature and a sense of wonder in being alive in this unimaginably diverse and immense universe. I only have to look up to the star-filled night sky to appreciate the greatness of the mystery of existence and my small place within it.

Mystics teach us that God - Buddha-nature - Brahman is implicit in all creation, including ourselves. That we are not separate from the Eternal. As the early Meister Eckhart, the great 14th-century German mystic, declared, God is the creator inseparable from creation: "God created all things not like other craftsmen so that they stand outside of himself, or beside himself, or apart from himself. Rather, he called them out of nothingness, from non-existence to existence... for he himself is existence."[1] and again: "The eye with which I see God is the same with which God sees me. My eye and God's eye are one eye; and one sight, and one knowledge and one love."[2]

Willigis writes: "The mystic goes beyond Western dualistic thinking that separates God and the world, the natural and the supernatural, human and the divine. 'God and I are one,' says Meister Eckhart. God is the innermost part of the human being, the spark of the soul, the whole being. The human person is, therefore, a reality in which God manifests himself."[3]

1. Armand Mauer *Meister Eckhart Parisian Questions and Prologues* (Toronto: Pontifical Institute of Mediaeval Studies, 1975), 89.
2. Claud Field *Meister Eckhart's Sermons* (London: Allenson, 1909), 14.
3. Willigis Jäger *Timeless Eternal Wisdom* translated by Marie-André Horsthemke (Dublin: Logos Publications, 2014), 48.

The Eternal manifests itself in everything, including the fabric of evolution as the process itself—whether it's a flower, tree, animal, human, or galaxy. The divine flows through all creation in and beyond time and space. In Buddhism, this is the Dharmakaya, neither form nor formless, not one, not two. God is the Holy Mystery that pervades the whole of reality and beyond time and space—an incomprehensible ground of being.

Yet, we are part and parcel of this great mystery and have the innate capacity to experience this ground of being within ourselves. That is why the 13th-century Japanese Zen master Keizan Jokin urged his followers to realize their *innate mind-ground and dwell comfortably in their original nature*.[4] Such sayings of the mystics, along with their imagery and poetry, point us toward the Eternal within; naturally, they will differ according to religion, culture, and the times given. However, similarities exist; what Zen calls mind-ground is no different from what Christian mystics call the ground of being. Such symbolic language helps direct our attention toward transcending the narrow confines of the perceived self – who we think we are.

Many people think of Buddhism as an atheistic religion, but this is simply a misconception. The images are different, that's all. The immanent Zen Buddhist, Soyen Shaku, of the early twentieth century, who was instrumental in bringing Zen to the West, spoke clearly of this misinterpretation: "At the outset, let me state that Buddhism is not atheistic as the term is ordinarily understood. It certainly has a God, the highest reality and truth, through which and in which this universe exists. However, the followers of Buddhism usually avoid the term God, for it savors so much of Christianity, whose spirit is not always exactly in accord with the Buddhist interpretation of religious experience. Again, Buddhism is not pantheistic in the sense that it identifies the universe with God. On the other hand, the Buddhist God is absolute and transcendent; this world, being merely its manifestation, is necessarily fragmental and

4. For reference to Keizan's *Zazen Yojinki* For reference, see the podcast: https://zenstudiespodcast.com/keizan-zazen-yojinki/ & the same-named article https://antaiji.org/en/classics/english-zazen-yojinki/

imperfect. To define more exactly the Buddhist notion of the highest being, it may be convenient to borrow the term very happily coined by a modern German scholar, panentheism, according to which God is *One and All* (from the Greek Ἓν καὶ Πᾶν) and more than the totality of existence."[5]

Kabir, the great 15th-century Indian mystic, writes poetically:

When He Himself reveals Himself,
Brahma brings into manifestation
That which can never be seen,
As the seed is in the plant, as shade is in the tree,
As the void is in the sky, as infinite forms are in the void
So from beyond the Infinite, the Infinite comes;
And from the Infinite, the finite extends.

The creature is in Brahma,
and Brahma is in the creature:
They are ever distinct, yet ever united.
He Himself is the tree and the germ.
He Himself is the flower, the fruit, and the shade.
He Himself is the sun, the light, and the lighted.
He Himself is Brahma, a creature, and Maya.
He Himself is the manifold form, the infinite space:
He is the breath, the word, and the meaning.
He Himself is the limit and the limitless,
And beyond both the limited and the limitless is He,
the Pure Being.
He is the Immanent Mind of Brahma
and in the creature.

The Supreme Soul is seen within the soul.
The Point is seen within the Supreme Soul,
And within the Point, the reflection is seen again. [6]

5. Soyen Shaku *Zen for Americans* (La Salle, IL: Open Court, 1974), 25-26.
6. Rabindranath Tagore *Songs of Kabir* (New York: MacMillan and Co., 1915), 50.

II

Just as the Eternal is embedded in all of existence, so does the longing for reconnection to the Eternal reside in the human heart, though it may lay dormant. All things are bound together, for we cannot separate ourselves from reality. Yet individuality exists within the unity of things, for our lives only have meaning and fulfillment in relationship to the whole of life.

In his writing, Willigis speaks about this fundamental interrelationship of things in the following way: "The relationship between a person and divine life can best be explained by resorting to a concept first coined by Arthur Koestler: that of a holon. A holon is an (autonomous) whole derived from Greek, but a whole does not exist alone, for it is always a part of a larger whole. An atom, for example, is part of a molecule; a molecule is a whole created from atoms, but it is simultaneously also part of a whole cell; the cell, in turn, is part of a whole organism. Thus, nothing is exclusively a part or a whole; everything is both part and whole. The holon thus has two tendencies: It must exist in both its totality and partiality; it must maintain a relationship to the whole and its own identity. Otherwise, it disappears. The more it tends to one side, the more it loses the other side. If a holon cannot or will not maintain both its identity as a part and its integration with the whole, it dies and disintegrates into its parts. The atom has to be *open* for the molecule; the molecule must be *open* for the cell, and so on. The holon only has meaning and continued existence in a more extensive holon. This means we can only exist as human beings if we do not solely hold on to our identity but also fit ourselves into the larger reality we are a part of. Like all other holons, we are called on to transcend and go beyond ourselves."[7]

Mystics, like Willigis, emphasize that we are a part of the web of life on earth and that we are not born into this world but born from the world, just as leaves do from a tree. We are part and parcel of this unimaginable dance called life, and our lives on earth are a precious gift.

7. Willigis Jäger *Mysticism for Modern Times* (Liguori, Missouri: Liguori-Triumph, 2006), 83.

I find it sobering to know, as science teaches us, that 99.9% of all species that have ever existed on this planet are now extinct. Humankind's appearance is but one stage in the grand story of life on Earth. This very earth and sun will also disappear sometime in the distant future. For me, the transitory nature of life—this short lifespan—brings urgency to finding the Eternal. This is the nature of impermanence in our lives.

For centuries, the great mystics have used the image of an ocean and a wave to express the underlying theme of unity and individuality—or, one could say, the whole undivided and divided. The sea symbolizes the Eternal, the primary reality; the wave is a temporal manifestation within this timeless reality. Our lives are akin to a wave, and yet we have the potential to experience both that *I am the wave* and that *I am part of the ocean.* And to mystics, there is yet another experience, of which Willigis writes: "When the wave experiences that *I am the ocean,* there is still two: wave and ocean. In mystical experience, even this duality is transcended, wherein the 'I' of the wave becomes blurred, and instead, the ocean experiences itself as a wave. It experiences itself *in* the unity of both and *as* the unity of both. The mystic does not take this step; the step happens to him."[8]

The mystic Kabir uses the image of river and wave to express this relationship poetically:

The river and its waves are one surf:
Where is the difference between
the river and its waves?
When the wave rises, it is the water,
when it falls, it is the same water again.
Tell me, sir, where is the distinction?
Because it is named a wave,
shall it no longer be considered water?
Within the Supreme Brahma, the worlds
are being told like beads:
Look upon the rosary with the eyes of wisdom.[9]

8. Willigis Jäger *Mysticism for Modern Times* (Liguori, Missouri: Liguori-Triumph, 2006), 13.

III

There are many pathways to mystical experience; for some, the mystical way is found through religious and spiritual traditions. Others seek and find transcendence through sports and athletic pursuits or artistic disciplines such as art, poetry, music, and dance. Yet again, some people have encountered transcendent experiences when opening up to great love or joy. Others may find mystical and spiritual experiences in the majesty of the natural world. In whatever circumstance we slip past the boundaries of self, mystical experience awaits, for it is inborn in the fabric of human life. Yet, we may not recognize those experiences for their transformative potential when they happen, and if we do, we may need to learn how to continue cultivating them.

American psychologist Abraham Maslov (1908-1970) referred to mystical experiences as *peak experiences* [10], which have a sense of wonder, awe, ecstasy, and a feeling of oneness with everything. At the same time, there may be a heightened sense of awareness and a timeless quality present. Naturally, many people readily interpret these experiences according to their religious understanding, yet, for others, such experiences may not be anchored into any religious context. Maslow believes that all people can have such moments while self-actualizing people (those who strive towards or live within their potential) will likely experience them more often.

The Benedictine monk and writer David Steindl-Rast writes: "In peak experiences, we glimpse what life could be like if humans were relating to one another and to all there is, not in an atmosphere of alienation but out of a deep sense of belonging. All of us are challenged by the glimpses we catch in our best moments. Those who rise to that challenge become mystics. Remember how these glimpses surprise us when we least expect them? Thomas Merton suddenly felt one with all on a street corner in Louisville, Kentucky, when he had merely set out to go to the dentist. He wrote, 'In Louisville, at the corner of Fourth and Walnut, in the center of

9. Rabindranath Tagore *Songs of Kabir* (New York: MacMillan and Co., 1915), 57.

10. Abraham Maslow *The Farther Reaches of Human Nature* (New York: Esalen Book, 1971), 190.

the shopping district, I was suddenly overwhelmed with the realization that I loved all those people, that they were mine and I theirs, that we could not be alien to one another even though we were total strangers. It was like waking from a dream of separateness, of spurious self-isolation in a special world, the world of renunciation and supposed holiness."[11]

Peak experiences are closely related to concepts such as Being in the Zone, Being in the Flow, or Superfluidity in sports, dance, or martial arts performance. Christopher Bergland, retired ultra-endurance athlete and writer, coined the concept of Superfluidity[12], which he said was a term he borrowed from the world of quantum physics to describe the highest tier of being *in the zone,* which "feels almost like an out-of-body flow state—in which thoughts, emotions, and actions synchronize with absolutely zero friction, viscosity, or entropy—and one's body and mind seem to perform effortlessly." Bergland noted that the psychological mindset accompanying superfluidity is marked by ego-less exuberance, a sense of connectedness to something much bigger, and pure joy.

These transcendent experiences are equally well known in the creative fields, as attested by artists, poets, musicians, and performance dancers throughout the ages. Indeed, any form of human creative expression can convey spiritual understanding and experience. Artistic expression can also provide a means to practice and enter transcendent and mystical experiences. To the mystic, the urge to create comes with a necessity to express the inexpressible ground of being. When we interact with great works in various art forms, we can experience transcendent spiritual moments—such as listening to music or poetry, viewing art pieces or sculptures, participating in dance, and so on.

Much conscious and unconscious spirituality is evident in the varied disciplines of creative expression throughout history. This can be seen in such classical examples as Zen calligraphy and gardens in Japan, the

11. David Steindl-Rast *The Way of Silence* (Cincinnati: Franciscan Media, 2016), 21-22. Including an embedded quote from Thomas Merton's *Conjectures of a Guilty Bystander* (New York: Image, 1968), 153.

12. Christopher Bergland *The Athlete's Way: Sweat and the Biology of Bliss* (New York: St. Martin's Press, 2007) & article *Transcendent States Assist Peak Performance in Mystical Ways* Internet source: www.psychologytoday.com

Sufi's dervish whirling in Turkey, the religious iconography of the Eastern Orthodox Churches, the Tantric paintings of India and Tibet, the Afro-Brazilian trance dancing of Candomblé, Gregorian chanting of Christian monks, the universality of religious architecture and sculpture, Navaho sand paintings, Balinese Calonarang village trance dramas, the world's sacred writings and spiritual poetry. This is a short list of humanity's uncountable creative spiritual expressions and practices.

In more modern times, we see spiritual creativity represented and explicitly acknowledged in various disciplines, such as in the jazz music of spiritual universalist John Coltrane (1926-1967), who said: "I'd like to point out to people the divine in a musical language that transcends words. I want to speak to their souls."[13] or the Zen-influenced music of Leonard Cohen (1934-2016) to the transcendental art of Vasily Kandinsky (1866-1944), Georgia O'Keethe (1887-1986), Hilma of Klint (1862-1944), and Joseph Beuys (1921-1986), who believed that one of the functions of art is to transcend the ego; to name but a few of the 20th-century master artists.

All of life's expressions of creativity can be vehicles for spiritual contemplative practice, either in their making or interaction with, for such works of art can express our deepest essence, mend our broken psyches, inspire us, lift our spirits, give us new perspectives of understanding, and transform our spirituality. This has been a limited survey of the immensity of spiritual and mystical art. However, the fundamental point is acknowledging that art can lead us to step past our limited self to a transcendent experience.

IV

Another pathway to mystical experience lies in the pure pursuit of knowledge and truth, which can be found in scientific inquiry of the highest order. When such a pursuit occurs, untainted by prejudice, it can lead to a new understanding, profound realization, and spirituality. This

13. John Coltrane quote Internet source https://thecreativeecho.com/john-coltrane/

common ground between science and spirituality, especially in exploring the implication of human life and the nature of this unimaginable universe, leads to the heart of what the mystic seeks: answering the mystery of one's existence. In this respect, science is akin to what Vedanta calls Jnana Yoga, the path of self-knowledge that leads to unity and wholeness. In Zen Buddhism, we have the saying: *seeing things as they are*—i.e., the true nature of reality.

Max Planck (1858–1947), the German theoretical physicist who discovered energy quanta, which won him the Nobel Prize in Physics, says, "There can never be any real opposition between religion and science, for the one is a complement to the other."[14] And Carl Sagan (1934-1996), the famous American astronomer and science communicator, echoed a similar sentiment, saying *that science is not only compatible with spirituality; it is a profound source of spirituality.*[15] Indeed, new lines of inquiry and a broader perspective can arise when we recognize that the gulf between science and true spirituality need not exist.

Willigis was also keenly interested in science and frequently talked about its connection to mysticism and its role as a means of transcendence beyond thinking. He wrote: "I believe that the basic impulse for the future development of the spirit will come from the natural sciences. It's my hunch that we will experience a rebirth of metaphysics where physicists and biologists—not philosophers and theologians—will be the midwives, as it were. These are the people who, in the course of research on the basic principles of science, increasingly come to the limits of thought. They encounter a reality there that they can neither doubt nor understand using the tools of logic or analytical thinking. For example, the German physicist Max Planck realized one day: 'I have become devout because I thought things to their end and could not think any further. All of us stop thinking much too early.' And he wasn't the only one who had such an experience. In the process of their research, other scientists - Erwin Schrödinger, Wolfgang Pauli, Albert Einstein - have come ever closer to

14. Henry Margenau and Roy Varghese *Cosmos, Bios, Theos* (Chicago Open Court, 1992) 1.

15. Carl Sagan *The Demon-Haunted World: Science as a Candle in the Dark* (New York: Radom House, 1995), 29-30.

religion or to mysticism, to be more precise. We have the terse statement from Werner Heisenberg (1901-1976): 'The first drink from the cup of science makes you an atheist, but waiting at the bottom of the cup is God.'"[16]

Other scientists used mysticism and spirituality to inform and inspire their research and understanding, especially in physics. For instance, Fritjof Capra (1939-), the American physicist, systems theorist, deep ecologist, and author of *The Tao of Physics*, writes: "Modern physics leads us to a view of the world which is very similar to the views held by mystics of all ages and traditions."[17] He goes on to describe the various parallels between modern physics and Eastern and Western mysticism as found in the Hindu Vedas, in the Buddhist sutras, but also in the fragments of Heraclitus and the Sufism of Ibn al-Arabi, amongst others.

Another notable example in physics is J. Robert Oppenheimer (1904-1967), the American theoretical physicist who directed the Manhattan Project's Los Alamos Laboratory (which developed the first atomic bomb). He found inspiration and solace in the Hindu text the Bhagavad Gita, which he could read in Sanskrit, once saying it is "the most beautiful philosophical song existing in any known tongue."[18]

Albert Einstein (1879-1955), the most famous and consequential scientist of the twentieth century, wrote in *Living Philosophies* that "the most beautiful thing we can experience is the mysterious,"[19] which, for him, inspired authentic scientific inquiry. Einstein's spirituality was based on a profound sense of wonder and awe of the mystery of life and the universe and contemplating its apparent secrets. According to his colleague, the American physicist David Bohm (1917-1992), Einstein believed in a non-personal generative force that created the universe.[20]

16. Willigis Jäger *Mysticism for Modern Times* (Liguori, Missouri: Liguori-Triumph, 2006), 74-75.

17. Fritjof Capra *The Tao of Physics* 4th Edition (Boston: Shambala, 2000), 19.

18. James Hijiya *The Gita of J. Robert Oppenheimer* (Proceedings of the American Philosophical Society Vol. 144, No 2, June 2000), 123. & https://tamilnation.org/humanrights/Hijiya.pdf

19. Albert Einstein Et al. *Living Philosophies* (New York: Simon and Schuster, 1931), 6.

20. David Bohm interview with David Suzuki *The Nature of Things* (CBC Canada television, May 1979) For reference, see the transcript, Internet source: https://www.organism.earth/library/document/nature-of-things

Einstein also commented on the question of wholeness, human alienation, and religion when he observed that "humans were part of the whole, the Universe that is limited in time and space, and that we, humans, experience ourselves in thoughts and feelings as something separate from the rest of reality" going on to say that this feeling of apartness is "an optical illusion of consciousness, and the quest for liberation from its bondage is the object of true religion." And when we no longer nurture this illusion but transcend it, we attain inner peace.[21]

David Bohm, the author of *Wholeness and the Implicate Order*, explored and expanded Einstein's idea of wholeness further. He held a radical approach to quantum mechanics and proposed that wholeness and interconnectivity are the fundamental principles of reality. He believed the universe is not a collection of separate objects but a seamless web of interconnected relationships. This view, deeply inspired by the spiritual philosophy of Jiddu Krishnamurti, profoundly influenced his scientific thinking on human awareness, the nature of reality, and the relationship between science and spirituality.[20]

V

The beginnings of spiritual movements and religions emerge from peak mystical experiences. Brother David Stendl-Rast writes: "The religions start from mysticism. There is no other way to start a religion. But I compare this to a volcano that gushes forth, and then the magma flows down the sides of the mountain and cools off. And when it reaches the bottom, it's just rocks. You'd never guess that there was a fire in it. So, after a couple of hundred years, or two thousand years or more, what was once alive is dead rock. Doctrine becomes doctrinaire. Morals become moralistic. Ritual becomes ritualistic. What do we do with it? We have to push through this crust and go to the fire within it."[22]

21. Bryce Haymond *Einstein's Misquote on the Illusion of Feeling Separate from the Whole* article. Internet source: www.thymindoman.com/einsteins-misquote-on-the-illusion-of-feeling-separate-from-the-whole & Alice Calaprice *The Ultimate Quotable Einstein* (Princeton, NJ: Princeton University Press, 2010), 339.

22. David Stendl-Rast *Lunch With Bokara* Link-TV program (2005 Episode: The Monk and the Rabbi) Internet source Gratefuliving.org channel (www.youtube.com/@grateful_org)

Today, many people find it challenging to see the fire and aliveness within religious institutions and their teachings. However, some religious and spiritual paths remain open to this mystical dimension, such as Zen and other Buddhist traditions, Christian contemplatives, Sufism, Vedanta, and Taoism. In these traditions, we are encouraged to go on a spiritual and personal journey towards direct experience of the most profound truths.

As the Tibetan Buddhist Tarthang Tulku notes: "Reality is all-encompassing: the absolute nature is one. Although we may feel separate from the original uncreated reality—whether we call it 'God,' 'peak experience,' or 'enlightened mind'—through awareness, we can contact this essential part of ourselves."[23]

Nevertheless, religions can and still do play a fundamental role in many people's lives worldwide. If we find spiritual comfort and personal expression in them, we should celebrate and honor our religious affiliation and beliefs. This is especially true when they offer meaningful spiritual practices and encourage sound ethical guidance. Religions can also lead us to the mystical dimension, and each person must choose what fits them on the mystical path.

In mysticism, we must acknowledge that religion and spirituality differ, although much overlap exists. Spirituality generally refers to the personal meaning and the values you hold about that which is more significant than yourself—however you define or name that. And how you practice what you believe to be true in your life. On the other hand, religions are specific spiritual pathways that embody traditions, philosophies and ethics, rituals and ceremonies, and mythologies in pursuing one's faith. You do not have to be religious to be spiritual, and today, there are a growing number of people who are not religious but identify themselves as spiritual. In North America, about a quarter of all adults have no religious affiliation yet consider themselves spiritual.

Unfortunately, there is a growing disconnect between the various religions and churches (temples, synagogues, and so forth) and the public.

23. Tarthang Tulku *Hidden Mind of Freedom* (Cazadero, CA: Dharma Publisher, 1981), 81-82.

Perhaps a significant reason is that religious and theological teachings are often based on worldviews and images that are no longer meaningful or relatable to modern people. Another factor is that religions frequently compete with each other and proclaim sole ownership of spiritual truth and salvation, a view that alienates many people used to an ever-increasing diversity in modern society.

Despite the decline of religion in the West, there is a growing interest in personal spiritual practices that give meaning, solace, and fulfillment. This trend in personal spirituality can be seen in numerous secular movements that have arisen in the last century, both in organized and unorganized forms. For example, people are increasingly attracted to the spirituality of the twelve-step programs that offer hope and recovery through a personal connection with one's higher power, which is self-defined. There is also a growing resurgence of interest in the transcendent experiences found in the use of psychotropic substances (such as ayahuasca and peyote) as used in spiritual shamanic ceremonies and therapeutic settings for individuals.

All of these avenues in the pursuit of spirituality, understanding ourselves and the universe, and expressing our innermost reality, as shown in the above examples, point to an innate need to find meaning, understanding, and connection to something greater than ourselves. And that we're willing to search for it. This is part and parcel of what I call the mystic impulse, which lies, I believe, within us all.

These genuine mystical practices and the search for transcendent experiences speak to a need in modern humankind. They are necessary for revitalizing spirituality in religious life and those in secular life who seek a meaningful spiritual life outside of religious affiliation. The 20th-century Catholic theologian Karl Rahner put it bluntly when he said, "The Christian of the future will be a mystic, or he will not exist at all."[24] In other words, they will either have a dynamic, immediate, experiential relationship with God or be bereft of faith.

24. Karl Rahner *Christian Living Formerly and Today -Theological Investigations VII*, translated by David Bourke (New York: Herder and Herder, 1971), 15.

For mystics, the differences in identity, belief, and religious dogma fade when we glimpse this transcendent experience of oneness and its unifying force of love. Rumi, the 13th-century Sufi poet and mystic, exclaims:

I no longer recognize myself.

I am neither Christian nor Jew,
nor Zoroastrian, nor Muslim.
I belong neither to the East nor West,
nor to the land nor sea.
I am not of nature nor the heavens above,
neither of this world nor the next.

My place is the Placeless,
My trace is the Traceless.

I belong to the Beloved,
and have cast duality aside.

One I seek, One I know,
One I see, One I call.

So deeply intoxicated from Love's Cup,
I dance in Ecstasy. [25]

25. Attributed to Jalaluddin Rumi, abridged by Arnie Lade & Terence Buie from Reynold A. Nicholson's *Jalâloddin Rumi, Selected Poems from the Divani Shamsi Tabriz* (Cambridge, UK: Cambridge at the University Press,1898), 125-128. & for reference, see the Internet source https://archive.blogs.harvard.edu/sulaymanibnqiddees/2012/11/06/rumi-i-do-not-recognize-myself/

CHAPTER 4

On Becoming Whole

I

No matter your religious, spiritual, or philosophical beliefs, the markers of growth in spiritual life are love, compassion, empathy, forgiveness, transcendence, wisdom, creativity, a sense of belonging, resilience within difficulties, meaningfulness, morality, hope, and gratitude, to name a few. These qualities grow and come alive on the mystical journey; only you can cultivate them. The famous Indian sage of the early 20th-century, Swami Vivekananda, said: "You have to grow from the inside out. None can teach you; none can make you spiritual. There is no other teacher but your own soul."[1]

As mentioned, spirituality in the mystical traditions also involves transcendent experiences, going beyond the boundaries of the ego's self-identity. In doing so, we free ourselves to live fully and become the great potential that's inherent in ourselves. I recall Willigis saying it this way several times: "I became human for one reason, to be fully human. I am here because I am meant to walk this earth in this structure, at this time, in this place. I am an individual note in this symphony of God, which resounds in this universe and evolution. And my task is to resonate fully with it in the way I have become. But it's not the note that matters; it's the music that matters. This note can fade away, and it will fade away, but the music goes on."[2]

The theme of becoming a whole person (in German, *Ganz Mensch sein*) was one of Willigis's frequent topics; he once wrote: "A few weeks ago, a young journalist asked me about my life motto. I could tell from her eyes that she was expecting something high-spirited. When I told her my life motto

1. Swami Vivekananda *Complete Works of Swami Vivekananda Vol. V* (Reading Time - Kindle edition, 2019), 1973.
2. Willigis Jäger *Ganz Mensch Sein* (Holzkirchen, DE: Wege-Der-Mystik, 2006), audio CD

was 'To be fully human,' she initially forgot about pen and paper. Obviously, she had something completely different in mind. This is my conviction: I became human because God wants to be human in me—*He/It* wants to manifest itself in this form, at this time, in this place, on this insignificant speck of dust in the universe. Life is our real religion. The true religion is being human. God wants to be lived and worshiped in this way."[3]

On the mystic's path, we enter into a process of transformation that leads out of the ego tunnel to embrace life as it is, in the here and now. We learn to accept all the trials and tribulations of life and use them as fertilizer for growth. We recognize that the life we have been given is the Eternal's life—God's life, and that the singular purpose is to become a better version of ourselves, a true human being. Or, as Willigis says above, God wants to become human in us. And in the words of Teresa of Ávila, the 16th-century Christian mystic, "My life is the life which God has lived in me."[4]

Of all the qualities that are awakened and nourished as we walk the spiritual and mystical path, the most essential is love. By moving away from self-centeredness, we kindle the living flame of love for all things. In Christianity, this love is thought of as unconditional love (agape) and charity, while in Buddhism and Hinduism, it's referred to as loving-kindness and compassion. The terms may differ, but the essence is the same: a universal love that embodies empathy, understanding, and participation with others.

This love shines on all things with benevolence, judging no one, even loving those who regard themselves as your enemy. It is a high task indeed, and there is no shame in, at times, falling short of this ideal, for this is a spiritual journey. True love is tolerant and willing to look at people's collective well-being, needs, and aspirations. Yet, it also has room for differing opinions in a relationship, community, country, or religion.

When we recognize that we all share the same ground of being, which is the source of love and compassion, true reconciliation can occur. We become aware that another's suffering, longing, and essential needs are no different

3. Willigis Jäger *Aufbruch in ein Neus Land* (Freiburg im Breisgau: Herder Verlag, 2003), 99-100.
4. C.J. McKnight *Mysticism: The Experience of the Divine* (San Francisco: Chronicle Books, 1994), 18.

from our own. I recall Willigis saying, "Love is not a commandment, but the ground structure of the universe; without the openness of love, the cosmos could not exist."

The 11th-century Chinese Confucian sage Zhang Zai wrote the following words to describe this deep kinship and belonging with all things: "Heaven is my father, and Earth is my mother, and even such a small being as I find an intimate place in their midst. Therefore, that which fills the universe I regard as my body, and that which directs the universe I consider as my nature. All people are my brothers and sisters, and all things are my companions."[5]

We cannot exist meaningfully without love, which makes us truly human and engenders worth, connection, and belonging. And, what will be the legacy of our lives? In Willigis's words: "What we hold in our hands at the end of our lives are not our achievements and our works. First and foremost, we must ask ourselves how much we have loved. And, how open we have been to our fellow human beings—the language of love is the only language that all human beings understand."[6]

One ritual embodying this profound expression of love in Christianity is sharing bread and wine, commonly considered communion. I recall that in the Benediktushof community, the following words were spoken when giving out the celebratory offerings: *Bread is for life, and wine is for love*. For me, bread and wine are symbols of inner transformation. These symbols also acknowledge the awakening and nourishing of the common bond of love that we all share. The spiritual rituals of sharing food and drink are universal, found in all spiritual paths, and are as old as humankind.

II

The spiritual journey also entails recognizing and accepting our failures, shortcomings, and weaknesses as humans. There is no need to bypass life's

5. Wing-tsit Chan *A Source Book in Chinese Philosophy* (Princeton, NJ: Princeton University Press, 1963), 497. & online source https://luminaryquotes.com/quote/the-western-inscription/

6. Willigis Jäger *Über Die Liebe* -Artikel (Holzkirchen, DE: West-Östliche Eisheit Willigis Jäger Stiftung) video extract translated by Arnie Lade. Online source https://west-oestliche-weisheit.de/ueber-uns/veroeffentlichungen-willigis-jaeger

difficulties; the task is to learn and grow through them. This is the way of transformation and change. The most profound personal questions or koans of daily life (as they are called in Zen) are often unsolvable and unanswerable; they can be tightly held wounds, traumas, addiction, and spiritual uncertainties that demand from us a resolution that usually cannot be found through rational, psychological or emotional means. The path of the mystics teaches us that the answer to these conundrums lies inward, in the true self.

The following is a beautiful passage by the mystic Johannes Tauler that, in a very earthy way, expresses the mystical and contemplative approach to solving these deep personal afflictions:

The horse shat in the stable,
and although the manure is rank,
that same horse hauls its crap
with great dignity onto the fields,
where the beautiful wheat
and noble, sweet wine grows,
which would never have grown so,
were it not for the horse's manure.

Likewise, carry your crap
to the field of God's loving fullness,
with perseverance and diligence.
For these are your difficulties
that you cannot resolve,
nor let go of or overcome.
And lay down your crap
upon the holy ground,
out of which will surely grow,
in humble serenity,
a wondrous fruit.[7]

In the east, the same sentiment is expressed in the saying: *no mud, no lotus*. These inner difficulties are fertilizer for spiritual growth; they need not be avoided but honored. To avoid facing our problems, we risk driving them deeper into ourselves, resulting in more suffering. We meet these difficulties not by confrontation but by letting go of our ego-centered identity and attachments with inner faith and resolve. And by practicing positive virtues and precepts, we prevent further suffering. This process takes time to cleanse ourselves of our afflictions. And we, in time, can come to see that even our most significant perceived failures help us to grow in ways we could never have imagined.

As we become more intimate with our emotions and feelings, we recognize that they are just a part of ourselves but not the essential component, which is the ground of being. Emotions, feelings, and thoughts pass through us like white clouds against the vast blue sky. The challenge is to learn to feel them all and, simultaneously, not let them take us hostage. This is what detachment means: a state that brings calm and centeredness.

In his epic *Mathnawi*, the Sufi mystic Rumi compares our thoughts and feelings to the constant stream of uninvited arrivals in a guest house. He advises that being human involves recognizing and accepting all that comes to us, whether it be sorrow, sadness, depression, or anger. By welcoming and not pushing away what comes, we can "scatter the withered leaves from the bough of the heart, so that fresh green leaves might grow," which will, in time, let real joy and transformations come in from the *Beyond*. Rumi emphasizes the importance of gratitude in this process, advising that should sorrow (or other distressing thoughts and feelings) come again, meet them all with serenity, saying, "O my Creator, save me from their harm, and do not deprive me of what good may follow in their wake. Lord, remind me to be thankful and let me feel no regret after they pass."[8]

7. P. Ermin Döll *Der Weg der Meister II* (Dietfurt/Altmühltal: Meditationhaus St. Frazsiskus, 1988), 255. & see also Willigis Jäger & Beatrice Grimm *Die Flötedes des Unendlichen* (Holzkirchen, DE: Wege-Der-Mystik, 2009), 42. Translated by Arnie Lade.

8. Jalaluddin Rumi Mathnawi - abridged by Arnie Lade from Reynold A. Nicholson's The Mathnawí of Jalalu'ddin Rumi Book 5, Verses 3645-95 (Cambridge, UK: Cambridge at the University Press,1933). For a modernized version, see Coleman Barks *The Essential Rumi* (New York: HarperCollins, 1995), 109.

And as Rumi intimates, room is made for joy when we let go of sorrow. In doing so, we realize that feelings and thoughts are just a part of life, but not all of life—a part of self, not its essence—which is the ground of being. This profound understanding can give us solace to face adversity. Rumi's sentiments are echoed in the following words of the early 19th-century English poet and mystic William Blake, he writes:

Joy and woe are woven fine,
Clothing for the soul divine;
Under every grief and pine
Runs a joy with silken twine.
It is right it should be so;
Man was made for joy and woe;
And when this, we rightly know,
Safely through the world, we go.[9]

III

Becoming whole is a lifetime process of willingness, acceptance, awareness, and courage to change. After one notable and emotional Zen retreat a few years back in Kentucky, I purchased a handmade fridge magnet from a vendor at a public market as a reminder to let all my feelings flow and become transformed. The magnet read: *FEEL ALL THE FEELINGS.*

In my practice, if I am aware of a challenging feeling, my first step is to bow inwardly with gratitude and acceptance of their presence. The next step is to look at them and discern their validity and significance from moment to moment, or if necessary, to reflect on them later. Some feelings are just emotions passing through that do not snag the little self; they leave no lasting hold but pass through me just as a sensation would. But the ones that do catch and stay with me are the ones that usually have messages for me. They can be feelings of anger, fear, discomfort, guilt, and

9. William Blake extract from the poem *Auguries of Innocence* lines 56-62 from *William Blake - Selected Poetry* (Glasgow, UK: Oxford University Press, 1996), 174.

shame, to name a few. These are the ones that need investigating regarding my role in their emergence, their historical context, and how I can learn to do better next time.

We all have personal koans to face, many of which revolve around our emotional lives and harmful behavior patterns, all of which are embedded in the limited historical self. The mystical path is the journey from this small self towards a fundamental wholeness and integration that comes with the recognition and experience of the ground of being, our true self. The mystical path invites us to transcend our koans and allow our true nature to emerge, whereby love emerges unbidden as part of a new forward movement in one's life. This is not always easy or painless, but it is essential to progress. In the words attributed to the poet Rumi: "Your task is not to seek for love, but merely to seek and find all the barriers within yourself that you have built against it."

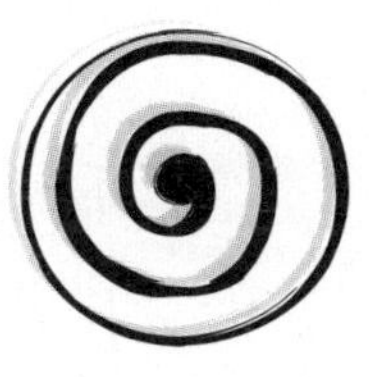

CHAPTER 5

Spiritual Precepts, Acceptance and Faith

I

In my life, the mystical journey has not led to a withdrawal from life but has led directly to a new intimacy with life. I have realized that freedom from suffering and spiritual awakening occurs within the very fabric of my ordinary daily life. The famous 20th-century German artist Josef Beuys once remarked: "The mystery is happening in the train station."[1]. And on this pilgrimage through life, the question arises about how we become more intimate with ourselves and embrace the moment wherever it finds us. And which spiritual practices and attitudes can best guide and sustain us? In this and the following chapters, I wish to explore how the mystical journey can be cultivated in everyday life.

To begin with, ethics is an essential component of living spiritually, one that all mystical traditions recognize as paramount to real progress. Huxley referred to the necessity of living virtuously (i.e., Dharma) in the first chapter. There is an old saying that *no matter how far down the road you go, the ditch always runs right along beside you*. This ditch represents all that is unfinished business, conscious and unconscious, that keeps us from recognizing the Eternal and separates us from our ground of being and our fellow human beings. We are in the ditch when we lose our moral and ethical compass. There, we'll find our deeply rooted desires, aversions, behaviors, and attitudes perpetuating and reinforcing the ego tunnel.

For example, when we engage in unkind, hurtful, or lustful behaviors, we inevitably harm ourselves and others. And the feelings that follow—shame, guilt, despair, fear, and many other thoughts and emotions—are bound to reinforce our sense of isolation and separateness. We become

1. Willigis Jäger *Mysticism for Modern Times* (Liguori, Missouri: Liguori-Triumph, 2006), xxxi.

further alienated from the Eternal and the immaculacy of the present moment.

On the other hand, when we resolve to uphold and train in ethical behavior based on spiritual principles, we move towards diminishing life's suffering and our sense of alienation that has come about through self-centered behaviors and attitudes.

Naturally, differing precepts or principles have arisen within and outside the great religious and spiritual traditions and the cultures they inhabit. Committing to one's chosen precepts, such as those found in Buddhism, Christianity, Vedanta, Sufism, and other world traditions, is most beneficial. These same core spiritual principles can also be found in secular recovery movements, most notably in Alcoholics Anonymous, Al-Anon, and all the Twelve-Step Programs that have followed in their footsteps.

The heart of all these spiritual principles, no matter what their source, is most clearly and briefly summarized in the Three Pure Precepts found within the Soto lineage of Zen Buddhist tradition, which are "Cease from evil, to do only good and to do good for others." as expressed by Zen Master Jiyu-Kennett (1924-1996).[2]

By following one's avowed spiritual principles and precepts, we actualize our fundamental desire to live in the fullness and interconnectedness of life. We become the best version of ourselves: compassionate, loving, whole human beings. We live without regrets, recognizing the sacredness of all things on this magnificent earth and incomprehensible universe. We open ourselves to an intimate sense of belonging to each other and creation.

And when and if we should fall into the *ditch*, whether it's shallow, deep, or muddy, we can get back on track through true humility, understanding our errors and remorse, making amends, and resolving to do better. In doing so, we slowly find new freedom from the constraints

2. Jiyu-Kennett *Roar of the Tigress* (Mt Shasta, CA: Shasta Abbey Press, 2005), 128.

of the past that bind us, helping our hearts widen their capacity for love and compassion for ourselves and others.

II

Willigis points out that the world's great ethical traditions arose from authentic spiritual experiences that awakened profound love. He writes: "Ethics don't have their origin in commandments. They belong to the basic structure of evolution. They amount to a natural law deriving from love. In the final analysis, ethics are nothing more than an agreement with the principle of transcendence and love. They are a result of an experience of God."[3]

And again, "The ethics of mysticism grow not out of intentions and appeals to the will, but from within and out of a deep experience of our being. Traveling the spiritual path transforms us to the core of our personality. This brings a transformation of consciousness and a view of the world that transcends the narrow circle of ego consciousness. In turn, the transformed personality gives rise to different purposes, values, and modes of behavior. We embark on a life of selflessness, wisdom, and compassion. An incontrovertible inner moral code comes into being... It is the code of love."[4]

For many, the mystical path is the beginning of a genuine moral understanding, an awakening to the profound interconnectedness of life, and a recognition that harming others or oneself affects us all. One's conduct is no longer based on social or learned morality but on insight, compassion, and understanding. We recognize the need to take responsibility for our actions, stop blaming others for our feelings or behavior, and seek healing and forgiveness for our past wrongs. In this way, we become free of regret, guilt, and shame and move toward wholeness and integrity. As a result of this process, selfishness, and self-

3. Willigis Jäger *Mysticism for Modern Times* (Liguori, Missouri: Liguori-Triumph, 2006), 120.
4. Willigis Jäger *Search for the Meaning of Life: Essays and Reflections on the Mystical Experience* Liguori, MO: Triumph Books, 1995), 196.

centered attachments and desires fall away, and love becomes the guiding principle of our lives.

Crucial to freeing ourselves of the past is the ability to forgive. Forgiveness is a spiritual act of opening our hearts and becoming free of the past, recognizing the inherent suffering of holding onto blame, anger, and hurt. Forgiveness often requires the courage to relinquish our attachment to a narrative of having been wronged by others or having harmed others ourselves. Yet forgiveness doesn't necessarily lead to reconciliation or even acknowledgment by the other person; it is, first and foremost, an internal act of dropping a position wherein we suffer for our inability to let go of blame and resentment.

The advice of a spiritual friend or teacher can be invaluable in discerning our role in a problematic situation where amends and forgiveness may be needed. We must also remain vigilant about attaching to a desired outcome or acting from a motivation that assuages our guilt.

A renewed and deepened understanding of spiritual ethics has been central to my journey, especially since meeting Willigis and walking down the mystical path with him. What I have learned from the practices of meditation and mindfulness has enriched my inner understanding and commitment to living by a higher moral compass. One continually refined and reinforced by the experiences of deepening love for others and a greater awareness of life and our profound interconnectedness. I live more fully when I see, acknowledge, and let go of selfishness, self-centered desires, and hurts in the past. As my awareness grows, my commitment to living ethically and morally, based on my chosen Buddhist precepts, helps me from ending up in the ditch!

III

In Buddhism, ethical and spiritual precepts facilitate the cleansing of karma, the repetitive cycle of actions and attitudes that only perpetuate suffering. When we refrain from harming and endeavor to help others, the conditions for awakening are cultivated. This is a demanding process with hidden challenges. As layers of selfishness, attachments, and other entanglements peel away, we inevitably face our most profound inner koans. At those times of internal crisis, our ethical and moral precepts stabilize the psyche to allow a transformation process to occur, which leads to a new understanding and awareness of our true nature.

In Christian traditions, abiding in a life of ethical morality and spiritual practice allows us to become aware of what separates us from fully receiving God's love and presence; this is called *the way of purification* in mysticism. Inevitably, we face what is fundamental to being human, including our relationship with the Eternal and the meaning of life and death (*resolving the Great Matter* in Zen).

Willigis remarks, "First, there occurs what the [Christian] mystics refer to as a process of purification. In psychological terms, you could also refer to it as a process of individuation in which the psyche becomes transparent for all the psychological blockages and conditioning developed through education, socialization, and religious education. Mind you, it's not a matter of casting aside those influences. It's more a matter of soberly assessing and accepting them for what they are. Our understanding transforms as our soul becomes transparent, especially in the religious sense. The God of Heaven, whom we prayed to as children, collapses. And many will then sigh, as Nietzsche did, and say, 'God is dead.' However, God is not destroyed; it's more a particular image of God that is destroyed.... This situation is a hard burden for many people to bear. They no longer know what to use as support. But this crisis marks the start of the next stage on the inner path of emptying the consciousness or unifying the consciousness, according to one's religious tradition or environment."[5]

Our commitment to the mystical path and spiritual ethics enables us to endure these challenges and whatever we encounter along the spiritual path. More importantly, we keep the temple of our hearts clean, not through willpower and self-denial but through our willingness to accept

5. Willigis Jäger *Mysticism for Modern Times* (Liguori, Missouri: Liguori-Triumph, 2006), 20-21.

whatever occurs along the way. We thus become open to letting go and stepping into the unknown, the mystery of our very being.

In his poem, *Letting Go*, Jim Quigley writes:

Everyday there is a letting go
some large, some small
some hard, some easy

With each comes an emptiness

A space left
for tomorrow's unexpected gift [6]

IV

The mystic recognizes that life, including one's own, is an expression of the Eternal. We are part and parcel of this cosmic mystery, and right here and now, we can fully participate in it, no matter the circumstance. This is not done by attaining or grasping with one's willpower but rather by letting go of selfishness and participating in life with sincere willingness and faith.

Willigis writes: "The tricky thing about the will is that it is tempted to make the matter of spirituality its own thing. It then becomes the ego's own declared goal to get rid of the ego. At this point, you are involved in a tricky paradox, for the will cannot give itself up. As long as you *want* to make progress along the spiritual path, you won't make any. Only the person who can let go of the will makes progress."[7]

Along the mystic's journey, trust in life and the ability to let go are the prerequisites for experiencing and abiding in the ground of being, the Unborn in and around us. Willingness is the key to the right effort rather than exerting willpower. A willingness to let go of one's selfishness and

6. Jim Quigley *Glimpses: Fifty Poems* (Nelson, BC: Crystal Mountain Publishing, 2016) Published with permission from author & publisher.

7. Willigis Jäger *S Mysticism for Modern Times* (Liguori, Missouri: Liguori-Triumph, 2006), 99.

accept things, ourselves and others as they are, even in difficult situations. Not to condone harmful behaviors and attitudes but to acknowledge their reality and effects. A willingness to keep our hearts open to love and compassion. It may be as simple as bowing and surrendering to what life has presented us in the very moment. And it may not be easy, but it is possible.

Willigis writes: "In the willingness to surrender, the new can unfold, and the process of maturation takes place, a process of becoming totally whole in our lives. This experience led the Zen master Ummon to say: 'Every new day is a good day.' A good day manifests itself in joy, pain, searching, and finding, in life and death beyond all opposites. A good day means enjoying life but equally letting go of things when they are gone. On a good day, we experience the mortality of life as an aspect of the whole of creation."[8]

We learn to accept that which we cannot alter. It may be our living situation, aging bodies or declining health, complex relationships, the changing environment, or social crisis. And yet, each day, we can better ourselves and help others, not by exerting willpower and forcing outcomes, but rather through a willingness to live according to spiritual principles. This, however, does not mean passivity or inaction along the spiritual path; action may also be required to do the next right thing. Indeed, making sufficient effort is essential to any progress, but believing one's will is the transformative power only seems to lead to frustration, for the self cannot transcend itself. I take great inspiration from the words of the Serenity Prayer: *God, grant me the serenity to accept the things I cannot change, the courage to change the things I can, and the wisdom to know the difference.*

8. Willigis Jäger *Timeless Eternal Wisdom* translated by Marie-André Horsthemke (Dublin: Logos Publications, 2014), 11.

V

Willingness also requires faith and a desire to examine one's most deeply held koans, beliefs, attitudes, and behaviors. As well as an intention to let go of what is no longer meaningful or harmful and unnecessary to become fully human and transparent to the Eternal. This requires living without demands on oneself, others, and life, in the words of Meister Eckhart, *to live without why.* This is elegantly expressed in the celebrated aphorism of 17th-century Christian mystic Angelus Silesius: "The rose is without any why; it blooms because it blooms. It does not look at itself or ask if it is seen."[9]

Yet faith does not mean unquestioning belief or abdicating one's discernment. Instead, it involves having confidence in spiritual teachings and considering the advice of wise teachers and spiritual friends who accompany you. Trusting that one's efforts will, in time, bear fruit is significant when encountering adversities. Faith means wholeheartedly taking up spiritual life and practicing as fully and deeply as possible. Faith, in turn, relies on purity of intention and wisdom.

Faith also means thoroughly recognizing that one's everyday life situation is where awakening is possible, and we do not need to be anywhere different, unique, or spiritual to find the Eternal. One day, the famous 20th-century Buddhist master Xu Yun (Empty Cloud) was asked, "The world is changing fast; where should I go to maintain my practice?" He replied, "To the student of the Tao, his home is everywhere, and if you only lay down everything, the place that you are is a *Bodhimandala* (place for realizing the truth). Please set your mind at rest."[10]

Faith involves acknowledging that we cannot know with certainty what lies ahead or that we have made the right decisions or taken correct actions. Yet, we can trust that our sincere efforts, desire, and willingness will lead to an awakening of the Eternal within us. A recognition that

9. Maria Bohm *Angelus Silesius' Cherubinischer Wandersmann* (Frankfurt: Peter Lang, 1997), 104.

10. Charles Luk *Empty Cloud: The Autobiography of the Chinese Zen Master Xu Yun* (London: Element Books, 1988), 137.

we are part and parcel of the life of God, which is the very ground of being (our Buddha-nature), and it is that very same ground that calls us to participate and experience the Eternal, the Unborn, in this life. Such faith will surely deepen our love and compassion for all.

The theme of will, particularly God's will, was central to a profound teaching and experience I once had with Willigis during a summer retreat. I struggled to discern the Eternal's will for me, a question that emerged unbidden from deep within after several days of intensive meditation. So, I brought this question of will to my following interview with Willigis, and during our discussion, I asked him if he thought we could know God's will for us. He replied, "No one could ever truly know God's will!" His answer surprised me and left me with a deep sense of doubt that grew over the following hours until it erupted into an intense spiritual experience as I sat in the meditation hall late into the night. This was an experience I could not adequately put into words; I can only say that there was a profound embodied sense of joy, surrender, acceptance, and being embraced by the Eternal—one that lingered in the days that followed.

CHAPTER 6

The Sacrament of the Present Moment

I

In spiritual life, meditation and mindfulness help me become more aware and alive and, in time, more fully present and connected to the ground of being and realize the Eternal within me. Most mystical, spiritual paths emphasize meditation and mindfulness as foundational practices for developing and transforming our awareness and perception of reality. In this chapter, I wish to explore these two aspects of awareness training, meditation, and mindfulness, in a general way, according to my understanding.

Willigis writes: "Mindfulness is the heart and starting point on the spiritual path. Leading a life of mindfulness means realizing that the true reality can only be experienced in the here and now. In order to get in contact with this reality, it is essential to practice mindfulness. The practice of mindfulness teaches us to be fully alive in every moment of life, so we can take full advantage of every moment."[1]

In Christian mysticism, mindfulness is described as the *sacrament of the present moment* by Jean-Pierre de Caussade in his 18th-century treatise on spiritual guidance.[2] Meditation and mindfulness are also at the core of Buddhist training, especially in the Zen tradition that I know. They are also implicit within Yoga, Vedanta, Sufi, and Taoist practices. Indeed, all authentic mystical traditions use forms of mindfulness, meditative, and spiritual awareness practices emphasizing becoming fully present, accepting life as it is, and acting wisely according to circumstances. These practices encourage us to let go of the unessential, the past that binds us,

1. Willigis Jäger *Timeless Eternal Wisdom* translated by Marie-André Horsthemke (Dublin: Logos Publications, 2014), 27.
2. Jean-Pierre Caussade, translated by Kitty Muggeridge *The Sacrament of the Present Moment* (San Francisco: Harper Collins, 1989)

the conditioned historic self that forms the roots of our suffering. And in this way, we learn to open ourselves to the deeper impulses of the life process.

Eventually, with continued meditation and mindfulness practice, inner stillness emerges, where we find moments of renewal, healing, and joy. Moments of awakening can arise too, without our effort, simply by letting go into the ever-flowing present moment—the *eternal now,* as Paul Tillich, the 20th-century Christian theologian, called it. Brother David Steindl-Rast reminds us that "the now is not in time; rather, time is within now."[3]

II

During the summer training at Benediktushof, one of my fondest memories was listening to Willigis leading a guided meditation. My favorite was a guided meditation called The Silence Behind the Silence, a narrow translation of the German *Die Stille Hinter Der Stille*. The German word *Stille* is a linguistic cousin of the English *stillness.* The modern German word and its old English form mean quiet, tranquillity, calm, silence, and abstention from speech. These same qualities help facilitate deep meditation, just as silence and tranquillity are beneficial environmental criteria for meditation.

We also find a parallel of these qualities emphasized in Zazen (Zen sitting meditation), especially in the Silent Illumination method, sometimes translated as Serene Reflection. Both names originate from the term *mò zhào* in Chinese and consist of two characters (默照): the first one translates as silence and serenity, and the second character means illumination or reflective awareness. Another popular Buddhist method, *samatha-vipassana,* contains similar elements: serenity and calmness (*samatha*) with insight or clear perceiving (*vipassana*).

3. David Steindl-Rast *i am through you so i* (New York: Paulist Press, 2017), 76.

Willigis wrote: "The silence is an incomprehensible presence. We are like a vessel that receives this silence until the vessel also disappears, and only silence remains. It has always been there!"[4]

Or, as the Christian mystic John of the Cross put it, silence is God's first language. In *Sayings of Light and Love,* he says, "The Father spoke one Word, which was his Son, and this Word he speaks always in eternal silence, and in silence must it be heard by the soul."[5]

Mystics like Willigis teach that this quality of silence and stillness found in meditation must become internalized and independent of externals so that mindfulness, attentiveness, and awareness become natural activities. In doing so, we move closer to the ground of being, our true nature.

Richard Wagamese (1955-2017), a treasured Canadian Indigenous author, reminds us that true silence goes beyond the mere absence of words. It involves addressing a deeper yearning to feel truly alive, beyond thinking, and above anxiety and frustration. Such silence embodies a state of calm in which we can cherish each moment as it is. And that each breath is a link to one's life's energy and essence.[6]

Indeed, when we practice, one of the easiest ways to sense, quiet, and connect to ourselves as embodied beings is through the breath. Natural, unimpeded breathing helps harmonize the entire body while stabilizing and settling consciousness. Simply following the breath with awareness can afford inner stillness and relaxed alertness. The more one practices such natural breathing, the more settled, whole-bodied, and quieter one becomes.

Furthermore, following the breath helps slow the stream of thought and can be used as a reference point to return to when carried away by

4. Willigis Jäger *Stille Hinter der Stille* (Holzkirchen, DE: Wege-der-Mystik, 2013), audio CD

5. David Lewis *The Living Flame of Love by St. John of the Cross (New York: Cosimo, 1912)* Kieran Kavanaugh & Otilio Rodriguez *The Collected Works of St. John of the Cross.* (Washington: ICS Publications, 1991), 92. Also see David Lewis *The Living Flame of Love by St. John of the Cross* (New York: Cosimo Inc., 1912 - Kindle edition 2007), location 2157.

6. Richard Wagamese *What Comes From Spirit* (Madeira Park, BC: Douglas & McIntyre, 2021), 25.

thoughts, strong feelings, or sensations (such as pain). We can trust the breath will be there to return to and ground us when needed. With practice, inner stillness helps the usual flow of thoughts, feelings, and sensations to pass through our awareness unimpeded when we refrain from controlling, avoiding, or clinging to them. We can learn to detach from the constant fixation on our thinking by letting them go—for our awareness is boundless and much vaster than they are. Thoughts, feelings, and sensations can be seen simply as passing clouds which neither obstruct nor alter the clear blue sky (of pure awareness) that lies behind them. Our awareness is the entryway to the ground of being, our truest abode.

During my retreats with Willigis at Benediktushof, I appreciated that he brought embodied awareness into his guided meditations. It helps bring oneself into the here and now—this place, this moment! Willigis often repeated that the body is our partner and friend on the spiritual path. That spiritual life begins in the body; it is there that the encounter with divine reality occurs. He often said that thoughts limit us, while the physical body can open us to more comprehensive awareness.[7] This reminds me that consciousness is physically embedded, that I am an embodied, spiritual being! Yet, I cannot ignore their differences. As the 20th-century Zen master Suzuki Roshi put it, *mind and body are not one, not two*!

All manner of interactions in our mind-body can happen in meditation. At times, I can be fully absorbed in thoughts, while at other times, physical sensations dominate. A merging of mind and body can also appear, or a subtle diffusing of both! On the journey to awakening, there can be a letting go or *dropping of mind and body,* as the great 13th-century Zen Master Dogen called it. Words fail to capture all the variations and dynamics of mind-body experiences in meditation.

7. Willigis Jäger & Beatrice Grimm *Der Himmel in Dir* (München: Kösel-Verlag, 2009), 17. & Willigis Jäger - editor Christoph Quarch *In Jedem Jetzt ist Ewigkeit* (München: Kösel-Verlag, 2003), 23.

III

Meditation, mindfulness, and contemplation exist throughout the world's great spiritual traditions. I wish to describe Willigis's basic outline of how they fit together and how we can use them. Of course, this is also based on my experience and understanding.

Willigis called meditation in the Christian context Contemplation. This is because meditation in Christian literature and teachings refers to discursive reflection, for example, on a scriptural passage. Contemplation, on the other hand, is when such reflective thinking ends, and interior silence is entered that leads to the presence of God. Contemplation is an integral part of the way of illumination taught by the Christian mystics.

On the other hand, Willigis generally used the term meditation when discussing Zen or other Eastern spiritual practices.

I find it interesting that the historical Buddha used the word cultivation (*bhāvanā* in the ancient Pali language) to describe practices of meditation, mindfulness, and other awareness training methods. For me, cultivating gives an image of planting, growing, nourishing, and harvesting cycles, which seem wonderfully aligned with a mature concept of spiritual practice. The modern Buddhist teacher Thich Nhat Hanh expresses this sentiment elegantly when he says: "Each time we practice sitting meditation, walking meditation, awareness of breathing, loving speech, deep listening, or any other mindfulness practice, our roots are growing stronger and deeper, and we are gaining more solidity and strength."[8]

Most people associate sitting with the ideal meditative posture, where the spine is relaxed, comfortable, and upright, whether in a chair or on the ground. However, meditation should be applied to more than just sitting. Any position can be used to meditate, including lying down, which is most useful when we're too ill to sit in the seated meditation position. Depending on the tradition in which meditation is taught, there

8. Thich Nhât Hanh *Fidelity: How to Create a Loving Relationship That Lasts* (Berkeley, CA: Parallax Press, 2011), 97.

are often specific recommendations, such as whether the eyes remain open or closed, how the hands are to be held, the placement of the legs and feet, and so forth.

Aside from body posture, Willigis taught that in formal meditation, there are two fundamental methods for entering interior silence and moving toward the ground of being. These two methods consist of gathering and emptying the stream of consciousness. They are the most common meditative methods in Christianity, Zen, and mystical traditions. Gathering consciousness naturally leads to emptying.

The first method, gathering, involves focusing on a specific point, such as your breath, a word or phrase, a sound, an image, or physical sensations. According to Willigis, Zen practice often starts with the breath or the koan *MU*, while Yoga emphasizes the sacred syllable *OM* or breath awareness. Sufi traditions may use the mantra *Allah Hu* or engage in whirling dance. Terms like Jesus, *Shalom*, or the simple Jesus prayer are common in Christian contemplation. The gathering method can also extend to walking, where breathing and sensing each footstep becomes the main focus. Eventually, with continued focus, this approach does lead to experiences of embodied unity and new levels of awareness.[9]

The second method, emptying, involves opening awareness to a broad, non-reactive state where attention isn't directed at any specific object. Willigis describes this state of consciousness as alert yet detached, functioning like a mirror that reflects without attaching to any image, whereby refined awareness allows us to withdraw from ego-driven activity, bringing stillness to our faculties. Through this method, the ego eventually quiets down so that one's true self emerges, resulting in a wordless and imageless perception of profound emptiness. According to Willigis, this emptiness has a distinct quality—a certain fullness that is much different than nothingness. In this method, the meditator remains passive, allowing their intellect and emotions to settle while detaching from specific thoughts, feelings, sensations, and imagery—and if they do arise, they are let go of and not followed.

9. Willigis Jäger *Ewige Weisheit* (München: Kösel-Verlag, 2011), 59-61.

In Zen, the emptying approach is known as *Shikantaza*, or sitting in silent stillness, while Tibetan Buddhism calls it *Dzogchen*, meaning the Great Perfection. It is also known as the *Prayer of Silence* in contemplation. These practices are intended to guide individuals toward experiencing emptiness, emphasizing attention to pure presence and awareness. An anonymous Christian mystic who wrote *The Cloud of Unknowing* describes this as looking into one's naked essence. [10]

Most people I know use only one of these methods in their practice. However, gathering and emptying can also be used complementarily. In the Christian contemplative tradition, a practitioner may start with the focused gathering method using a sacred word, a simple phrase, or an image, such as in Centering Prayer. Later, as the practice continues to deepen, one arrives at a place where focusing on words naturally drops away, and one becomes empty or *naked* to God's presence.

Many others and I sometimes use both the gathering and emptying methods in our Zen practice. I may start meditating by focusing on my breathing. Still, in a short time, I'll transition to practicing non-focused awareness of the emptying method, also referred to as *Shikantaza* or just sitting. My Zen Buddhist teacher, Rev. Master Meiten McGuire (1926-2018), referred to this emptying method of meditation simply as *sitting with awareness*.

Zen's *Shikantaza*, also known as Silent Illumination or Serene Reflection meditation, is a beautifully simple yet challenging practice at times. And how do we *sit with awareness*? As the great Zen Master Dogen wrote, "When a thought arises, be aware of it; when you are aware of it, it will disappear. Continuously set aside everything and become one with yourself."[11] Dogen later refined this instruction in his *Rules for Meditation* (Fukanzazengi), with the image of *nonthinking*, which the modern Zen Master Jiyu-Kennett skillfully interprets to mean that "neither trying to think nor trying not to think; just sitting, without any deliberate thought,

10. Willigis Jäger *Ewige Weisheit* (München: Kösel-Verlag, 2011), 59-61.

11. Tairyu Tsunoda *Hishriryo (Non-thinking)* Internet source https://www.sotozen.com/eng/library/key_terms/pdf/key_terms08.pdf

is the important aspect of serene reflection meditation."[12] The primary intention behind Shikantaza is to let go of whatever arises in the mind and not to cling to, follow, or suppress thoughts, feelings, or sensations. Instead, the focus is simply returning to and abiding by one's innate awareness.

Willigis writes: "Both [gathering and emptying] methods lead to a point where the ego realizes it isn't what it considered itself to be. Our ego identification falls apart, and we realize that our actual identification lies far deeper than our ego. We are on the threshold of an experience, pictorially described as where the wave no longer experiences itself as the ocean; it is now only ocean—unity without an opposite."[13]

Willigis once explained the essence of Zen meditation: "Sitting without a specific purpose means embracing doubt, boredom, and tiredness while maintaining your inner presence. This can involve focusing on the breath, contemplating a koan, or practicing Shikantaza. In this practice, eternity, timelessness, and the 'unborn' are always accessible. Ultimately, this is what 'awakening' signifies—experiencing the presence of timelessness in each moment, which makes every ordinary moment extraordinary. Through this awareness, individuals uncover benefits that are often concealed by the activity of ego consciousness. Nothing new is created; instead, people rediscover what has always existed. Those who turn inward connect to the very essence of everything that exists and, consequently, to all beings. This connection gives rise to a bond we refer to as love."[14]

Meditation is not a linear journey but a lifelong and deepening relationship with the most intimate part of myself. Whatever experiences I have had or will have are a combination of many factors, known and unknown; they are the harvest of my sincerity, willingness to continue, spiritual guidance, and simply grace.

12. Jiyu-Kennett *Serene Reflection Meditation (*Mt Shasta, CA: Shasta Abbey Press, 2016), 2.

13. Willigis Jäger *Mysticism for Modern Times* (Liguori, Missouri: Liguori-Triumph, 2006), 21.

14. Willigis Jäger *Ein Nichtbuddhist fragt Buddha – Nikodemus fragt Jesus* - Artikel (Holzkirchen, DE: West-Östliche Eisheit Willigis Jäger Stiftung). Internet source https://west-oestliche-weisheit.de/ueber-uns/veroeffentlichungen-willigis-jaeger)

It seems natural that our meditation experience evolves and changes as we let go of self-centered attachments and vexations, including holding on to any spiritual and transformative experiences we've had. There is no need to try to replicate, avoid or induce any experience; our ongoing practice is to return to *being present with awareness and letting go of the little self,* as Rev. Meiten would so often say.

In meditation, we face our innermost selves, including our historical memories, difficulties, struggles, and other parts of us that can lie deeply buried. Some parts may be shame-based or trauma-related, for example. Meditation is not a panacea for our problems, nor a reason to bypass them. The mystics tell us that the path to the true Self, the ground of being, requires a loving acceptance of our entire being, including the little self and all its parts. In meditation, profound healing and integration of unwanted aspects of ourselves become available and, in time, fulfilled.

This paradox is that to let go of the ego, the little self, I must also love and accept all the parts of myself to become whole. Then, those parts of me that cause me pain, grief, sorrow, and shame will dissipate and no longer cause such suffering.

The German Dominican mystic and contemplation master Johannes Tauler wrote:

If one remains in the practice of Contemplation,
the little self has no hold.
That self that wanted to have things,
that knew things,
that wished for things.
Until these things in him die,
Man faces bitterness.
This does not happen in one day
or in a short time.
One must persevere and, in time,
practice will be easy and satisfying.[15]

IV

When I first met with Willigis one-on-one, he asked me about my meditation practice. I replied I was using the Serene Reflection method that my Zen teacher, Rev. Master Meiten, taught. We also talked about formal koan study, but after some discernment, he advised me to continue my current practice. I later understood that Willigis's advice was an exception because most of his Zen students did formal koan studies with him, but he never advised me to do the same. Nevertheless, let me say a few words about koans and how they are used since there is so much lore about them in Zen, and they are often misunderstood.

The word koan (gōngàn in Chinese) originally meant a public record (as in the public records of a law court). In the Zen tradition, koans refer to the many historical dialogues and sayings of imminent Masters and their students, recorded with commentaries by later Masters and compiled in texts such as the Blue Cliff Records, the Records of the Transmission of the Lamp, and the Gateless Gate.

Koans express the awakened mind of the Zen master; they also reveal the catalyst for an ancient master's enlightenment, and they are used as a teaching device by a Master to help a student realize their true nature. Most koans are seemingly enigmatic and cryptic but contain pointers to Zen Buddhist truths and doctrines that embody skillful means to expedite a practitioner's awakening (kensho). In general, koans have three practical applications in training: as an object of focus in meditation, as an in-depth instructional and training process, and as a self-inquiry agent involving the fundamental questions that arise in one's life. As a practice, resolving any particular koan cannot be done by one's reason, will, or memory but instead through intuition and insight.

Just one word or phrase is most frequently used as an object of meditation, such as Mu, which Willigis used extensively with his students. In Chinese, the word Mu or Wu means no, not, non-being,

15. Ermin Döll *Der Weg der Meister* (Dietfurt/Altmühltal: Meditationhaus St. Frazsiskus, 2005), 243. & see also Willigis Jäger & Beatrice Grimm *Die Flöte des Unendlichen* (Holzkirchen, DE: Wege-der- Mystika, 2009), 44. Translated by Arnie Lade.

and nothingness—as in spiritual Emptiness. This word Mu comes from the well-known Koan dialogue between Master Zhaozhou and a monk who asked him: "Has the dog Buddha-nature or not?" to which Master answered, "Mu!" Nowadays, practitioners meditate on Mu to fully penetrate and become one with it (in body, mind, and spirit) to arouse a kensho experience. It is often the first koan given to a student in many Zen schools.

In certain schools of Zen in Japan, koan study with a Master involves a curriculum of hundreds of classical koans for the student. Often, this begins after the student has had a kensho experience with the Mu koan. The teacher uses the classical koans to check students' understanding and depth of experience and to deepen the practitioner's initial kensho and spiritual maturity. Willigis studied in a school in Japan that blended both koan-focused training and Shikantaza meditation, including a rigorous curriculum of hundreds of koans.

However, in Zen, there is another common approach to koan study. This is what the great Master Dogen called the Genjokoan, the koan of everyday life. It arises as a spiritual difficulty and impediment that is unanswerable and unsolvable for the limited, historical self, the ego-self.

This type of koan that arises naturally in life may have brought you into spiritual practice in the first place. The question might have been: Why is there suffering? Who am I? Why am I alive? Who dies? or some other irresolvable personal koan? These koans can also arise in one's spiritual practice in many forms, such as: Why am I always so angry? What is God's will for me? How can I be with this grief? Why do I feel so unloved? How can I stay married? And pretty much any seemingly challenging, vexing difficulty can bring forth a spiritual crisis. Such koans indicate a spiritual barrier one must face, penetrate, clarify, and transcend.

The study of the koans of everyday life informs my practice. They reflect what is alive in me and what spiritual barriers I need to work on. I use them to train.

Another way koans are used in Zen is by investigating the *hua tuo*, a common method in China today. Hua tuo means a word-head (referring to that which precedes a thought or spoken word). For instance, when one inquires, "Who is reading this?" the moment before a thought arises about this question is the word head, and as soon as a thought or word occurs, it becomes known as a word tail (*hua wei)*. In this method, the word-head is a gateway to the unborn within us, the mind-ground, while the word-tail is none other than the discriminating mind of the limited, historical self.

Koans such as 'Who is dragging this body around?' 'Who is hearing?' or 'Who is repeating Buddha's name?' are frequently used as sources for these word-heads. The emphasis is given to one word, 'Who?', which the practitioner firmly focuses on and inquires into while letting go of all else. The point is to enter the gap between thoughts using the light of our awareness.

The venerable 20th-century Master Xu Yun, speaking about the method, said, "In a clear sky, when the sun rises, and sunlight enters (the house) through an opening, the dust is seen moving in the ray of light whereas the empty space is unmoving. Therefore, that which is still is voidness, and that which moves is dust. Foreign dust illustrates (false) thinking, and voidness illustrates self-nature... The moment before a thought arises is called the *Unborn*. That void that is neither disturbed, dull, still, nor one-sided is called the *Unending*. The unremitting turning of the light inwards on oneself, instant after instant, and exclusive of all other things, is called looking into [investigating] the hua tou."[16]

In the Indian teachings of Jnana Yoga, there is an approach to self-inquiry reminiscent of the Zen method of hua tuo. The eminent 20th-century spiritual master Ramana Maharshi asked his disciples, "Who am I?" as a method of meditative self-inquiry. Willigis once commented that we do not see things in their true form because of the ego's way of knowing conditions us. He explained that by persistently contemplating a koan or question such as "Who am I?" we push aside all other thoughts

16. Lu K'uan Yü *Ch'an and Zen Teachings - Series One* (London: Rider & Company, 1969), 37.

and conditioning, allowing the ego's grip to loosen and, eventually, our true selves to be revealed.[17]

Similarly, the 20th-century Jnana teacher, Sri Atmananda Krishna Menon, used the image of the gap between thoughts. Joseph Campbell, the renowned American mythologist and writer, wrote about his meeting with Sri Atmananda in the 1950s and the teachings he received, as follows: "Through quite a series of adventures, I managed to get an audience with this wonderful little man. He was seated in one chair, and I was in the other—this was quite a confrontation. Of course, the first thing he says is, 'Do you have a question?'

I learned later that I had the good fortune to ask exactly the question that had been his first question to his guru. The question I asked was this: 'Since all is Brahman, since all is the divine radiance, how can we say no to anything? How can we say no to ignorance? How can we say no to brutality? How can we say no to anything?'

To this, he said, 'For you and me, we say yes.' Then he gave me a little meditation—and it's a good one: 'Where are you between two thoughts?' You're thinking of yourself all the time, everything you do. You know, there's the image of yourself—your ego. So, where are you between two thoughts?

That's what that intuitive flash is giving you a taste of. This thought, that thought, the ripple of the mind—do you ever have a glimpse that transcends anything you could think of about yourself? That's the source field of which all of your energies are coming. And so the hero's journey through the threshold is simply a journey beyond the pairs of opposites, where you go beyond good and evil."[18]

This transcendence beyond all opposites, including the self, is aptly summarized in Dogen Zenji's famous saying: "To study the Buddha Way

17. Willigis Jäger - editor Christoph Quarch *In Jedem Jetzt ist Ewigkeit* (München: Kösel-Verlag, 2003), 79.

18. Joseph Campbell *Pathways to Bliss* (Novato, CA: New World Library, 2004), 115. Copyright © Joseph Campbell Foundation (jcf.org). Used with permission.

is to study the self; to study the self is to forget the self; to forget the self is to be actualized by myriad things."[19]

V

At Benediktushof, during retreats, seated meditation periods were twenty-five minutes long. This was a reasonable length of time for practice. A typical retreat day would consist of multiple sitting periods interspersed by walking meditation, work periods, meals, guided movements, rest, and formal talks. Practicing in a group helps keep one's awareness fresh, and it reminds us that we are not alone—that I am sitting with my fellows and, by extension, with all beings and things in this unimaginable universe in which the Eternal is always present. A universe where the ordinary is implicit within the wonder of existence. This is aptly stated in the Zen poem:

(As I) sit quietly, doing nothing. Spring comes, and the grass grows of itself.[20]

Zen also has *kinhin,* or walking meditation, which complements sitting meditation. It relieves the body of any strain from sitting meditation and refreshes the mind and body. Just as in sitting meditation, the methods of gathering or emptying are used when walking, thus allowing one's practice to flow seamlessly between sitting still and moving. Sometimes, however, it is helpful to change the object of their focus when walking, such as to the sensation of the bottom of the foot or the breath. This can be refreshing while grounding awareness through the body and the environment.

I have encountered many styles of walking meditation in different Zen traditions. At Benediktushof, both fast and slow walking were equally emphasized. Slow walking was mostly done with relaxed ease in the meditation hall between sitting meditation periods. On the other

19. Kabuki Tanahashi *Moon in the Dewdrop writings of Zen Master Dogen* (New York: North Point Press, 1985), 70.

20. Alan Watts with Al Chung-Liang Huang *The Watercourse Way* (New York: Pantheon Books, 1975), 43.

hand, fast walking was primarily held outdoors in the fresh air. We'd walk quickly and vigorously in a large circle, clockwise within the inner courtyard, first thing in the morning and repeated during the rest of the day.

Walking meditation can become part of our daily lives and can be done alone or with friends. Many people sense that it has a remarkable rejuvenating effect that connects and heals in a natural environment, such as the woods or along a river or seashore. I have also experienced that it's easier to intuit and feel something bigger, more significant than myself in nature, which affords me a more profound sense of kinship with life.

Thich Nhat Hanh, the eminent and influential Buddhist teacher, writes: "People usually consider walking on water or in thin air a miracle. But I think the real miracle is not to walk either on water or in thin air but to walk on earth. Every day we are engaged in a miracle which we don't even recognize: a blue sky, white clouds, green leaves, the black, curious eyes of a child—our own two eyes. All is a miracle."[21]

In the last few decades, there has been a resurgence of people walking pilgrimages for spiritual purposes. Walking routes such as the Camino de Santiago are being revitalized throughout Europe, as are many walking routes worldwide, such as in Japan, Ireland, and South and North America. Wherever we live, natural environments offer ideal places to walk. These places are our most ancient living cathedrals and holy temples where we can worship, meditate, and walk in with reverence.

VI

Zen and contemplative practices emphasize that the touchstone of spirituality is the here and now - in which being present, truly alive, and mindful of ourselves, others, and our environment is most important. In Zen, this is called every-moment mindfulness, the practice of being aware and awake. Meditation is fundamental to its development.

21. Thich Nhât Hanh *The Miracle of Mindfulness* (Boston: Beacon Press, 1976), 12.

Every-moment mindfulness can be practiced no matter the circumstance, such as washing the dishes, exercising or moving about, reading, speaking, falling asleep, or listening to a friend. Mindfulness occurs simply by being present and aware with wide attention and a loving intention—in a relaxed and gentle way with openness and a receptive heart. One of the easiest ways to enter into mindfulness is through gratitude, remembering the beauty and preciousness of people and things in our lives with all their blessings and gifts.

Also, specific reminders and aids can help us to remain or return to being present, especially when we become distracted, overwhelmed, or lost in thoughts or emotions. Focusing on breathing effectively returns us to the present moment. Other ways to return to presence include reciting a prayer, mantra, or meaningful phrase or taking time to make a sacred gesture such as bowing or simply pausing whatever we're doing.

In spiritual practice, every-moment of mindfulness is not a technique to gain something, like productivity or becoming less anxious, although this can occur. More importantly, it is a natural way to practice becoming aware, in tune with ourselves, and authentically available to others to foster love, connection, and wisdom. As the Dominican Friar Johannes Tauler once said: "In the school of the Spirit, man learns wisdom through humility, knowledge by forgetting, how to speak by silence, how to live by dying."[22]

22. Susannah Winkworth *The History of the Reverend and Doctor John Tauler* (London: Allenson & Co, 1905) Sermon XIX. Internet source https://ccel.org/ccel/winkworth/tauler/tauler.ii.html

CHAPTER 7

Prayer, Gestures and Rituals

I

Prayer has become increasingly important to me, especially as I move deeper into my elder years. It keeps me connected to the source in and around me. Even when challenged to articulate words, I can pray silently, put my hands together, and bow. For me, prayer is an essential aspect of spiritual practice, whether done with words, in silence, or as gestures with my body.

When we pray for someone or a situation, give thanks or praise, or beseech help or healing, or fortify our faith, we activate, as Willigis put it, "non-personal, cosmic energies that belong to evolutionary structures—in which love governs."[1]

I recall Willigis once explaining in a lecture that every blessing, prayer, chant, mantra, and sacred gesture—such as making the sign of the cross or bowing—sends out positive energy. He noted that while some might view them as mere magical acts, they actually represent a way of transmitting positive energy into the field of collective consciousness that surrounds and informs us. He also emphasized that when we offer blessings and engage in prayer, chants, and sacred gestures, we open ourselves to this larger field, which is fundamentally love.[2]

Mystics know that prayer, in whatever form, is a profound act of opening our hearts to the great Mystery, which we may call God, Buddha nature, or some other holy name. To pray is to live mindfully in the here and now, immersed in all the uncertainties of life, and yet keeping faith

1. Willigis Jäger *Geh den Inneren Weg* (Freiburg im Breisgau: Herder Verlag, 2019), 19.
2. Willigis Jäger *Das Leben endet nie* (Bielefeld: Theseus in Kamphausen Verlag, 2007), audio CD & Willigis Jäger edited by Christoph Quarch *In Jedem Jetzt ist Ewigkeit* (München: Kösel-Verlag, 2003), 129.

in the Eternal within us. And when we pray, we become closer and more intimate with life in and around us. We can learn to pray with our entire self—mind and body; all that is required is our right intention, attention, and heartfelt sincerity. We don't need to search outside of ourselves to make this connection. We can acknowledge with humility, as the Zen Master Jiyu-Kennett put it: "I am not God, and there is nothing in me that is not of God."[3]

The sacred source lives within us, and there within us is our true abode and refuge for prayer, as the Indian mystic Kabir reminds us in his poem:

O servant, where dost thou seek Me?
Lo! I am beside thee.
I am neither in temple nor in mosque:
I am neither in Kaaba nor in Kailash:
Neither am I in rites and ceremonies
nor in Yoga and renunciation.
If thou art a true seeker, thou shalt at
once see Me: thou shalt meet Me
in a moment of time.
Kabir says, "O Sadhu! God is the
breath of all breath."[4]

Prayer has been a part of human life since immemorial. Whether you are a Hindu, Jew, Buddhist, Christian, Muslim, or Taoist, or follow an indigenous spirituality or no formal path, prayer can be a source of insight and strength. Prayer can guide us to make appropriate choices and actions in our lives and avoid short-sighted and self-centered decisions that cause ourselves or others harm. Prayer can bring us peace of mind and express our gratitude, inspire love and compassion, kindle remorse, and foster forgiveness and acceptance. A life with prayer leads us along the contemplative path, one that compliments formal meditation and other

3. Jiyu-Kennett *Roar of the Tigress* (Mt. Shasta, CA: Shasta Abbey Press, 2005), 115.
4. Rabindranath Tagore *Songs of Kabir* (New York: MacMillan and Co., 1915), 45.

mindfulness practices, all of which lead us towards inner stillness, pure awareness, and the ground of being.

II

Prayer can take many forms, for we all know that our bodies can directly express love, gratitude, and spirituality as much, if not more, than words. For example, a loving touch, embrace, or heartfelt smile can be a profound expression of another that can lead to closer intimacy and connection. In the same way, in prayer, our bodies can directly express our innermost aspirations and feelings through reverential gestures, though wordless and free of thought.

During my stay at Benediktushof, this wordless and body-centered form of prayer was emphasized in a practice called Körpergebet (literally meaning bodily prayer). Körpergebet was developed by Willigis and Beatrice Grimm, his longtime student and fellow contemplative teacher at Benediktushof. This original and powerful contemplative practice incorporates and synthesizes sacred gestures from worldwide spiritual traditions. Often, during the summer training I attended, we would gather outside on the lawn and be guided through the flowing series of gestures and movements of Körpergebet. Some teachers at Benediktushof would lead us through their preferred mindfulness practices, such as Hatha yoga and Qi Gong.

Body-centered mindfulness plays a vital role in spiritual training. At all the retreats I attended at Benediktushof, and in the various Zen temples I've visited, the practice of awareness is implicit in walking meditation, bowing, full-body prostrations, working, religious ceremonies, and so forth.

Willigis taught that gestures are an indispensable and ancient way for individuals to connect with their true selves and divine origins. All religions incorporate meditative postures, movements, and gestures that enhance openness, allow energy to flow, and activate a strong transforming influence. In Christianity, various prayer gestures were used in monasteries long before they fell into relative obscurity. Prostrating or lying flat on the ground is a common form of devotion across all faiths. For instance, Jesus prostrated himself on the Mount of Olives, surrendering his life to God's will. In Zen Buddhism, practitioners often perform one hundred and eight prostrations. Similarly, Tibetan Buddhists take a pilgrimage around Mount Kailash, engaging in a continuous act of prostration. Followers of Islam also express their devotion by prostrating in prayer toward Mecca.[5]

In embodied practices, we put aside thinking and allow our awareness to be present in our actions. We become present by deeply listening, sensing, and perceiving ourselves without judgment or analysis as we move and act. This allows our awareness to grow with calmness and attention and gives us a path toward presence (fully living in the sacrament of the present moment). When we let go and be fully in the moment, an inner stillness and a felt sense of our true self arise.

Willigis writes: "Individual gestures affect the psyche. Above all, they change the religious self-image. Our self-image limits us because a large part of our personality is filled with beliefs and ideas imprinted on us from childhood and youth, often preventing us from truly living. They determine our religious life, relationships, feelings, and behavior at work and in society... When used regularly, gestures can help dissolve rigid boundaries and free us from self-centered conditioning, prerequisites for spiritual progress. If the old remains, there is no real change. Only those who can let go of identifying with their self-image, which continues into the finest nuances of the contemplative path, can reach the experience of emptiness and unity. In the gesture of prayer, much that was previously unconscious becomes conscious and can be processed and released."[6]

Willigis further explains: "Spiritual paths begin in the body: the lotus position in the eastern approaches, which assigns a particular posture to the head, neck, back and legs, with mudras of the hands are all symbolic gestures that combine an external pose with spiritual ideas; the asanas

5. Willigis Jäger *Über Die Liebe* (München: Kösel-Verlag, 2011), 68-69.
6. Willigis Jäger & Beatrice Grimm *Der Himmel in Dir* (München: Kösel-Verlag, 2009),14-15.

of yoga, physical poses that make you permeable; the dance turns of the dervishes and the body movements of the Sufis to the mantra Allah-Hu or the Rak'ahs (bows and prostrations) all show the importance of the body in mystical prayer. The body is the starting point. It is the vessel in which the encounter with divine reality is contained. Unfortunately, in Christianity, the importance of the body in spiritual life was almost wholly lost. The body is seen more as an obstacle, to be chastened and made subservient through asceticism. However, according to St. Dominic, there are many prayer postures in which the body plays an important role. In the Middle Ages, these gestures were still a natural part of prayer. Today, we only see them on certain occasions, such as religious ceremonies or ordination."[7]

In contrast, most Eastern religious traditions do not separate mind and body in spiritual practice. Thich Nhât Hanh, the eminent Vietnamese Zen teacher and author, writes: "In the Buddhist tradition, we learn that body and mind are not separate. The body is part of the mind, and the mind is part of the body... That is why, in sitting meditation, in walking meditation, in mindful work, in the practice of breathing, mind, and body become one, for the practice to be correct."[8]

Fundamentally, the foundation of all prayer is mindfulness, attention, and intention, no matter what form or activity it takes. Our everyday lives can become an act of worship, a prayer, where the distinction between verbal and non-verbal disappears. For example, walking becomes a mindfulness prayer that involves the whole self—mind and body. With each step, there's an opportunity to build and refine awareness through sensing yourself as you move, how you breathe, and how you are connected to your surroundings until you, the activity, and the environment become one. A sense of unity and continuity emerges. In such a way, all activities can become opportunities for silent prayer: having a cup of tea, standing at a bus stop, taking out the garbage, building a new fence, painting, or playing a sport are moments to practice mindfulness and presence.

7. Willigis Jäger & Beatrice Grimm *Der Himmel in Dir* (München: Kösel-Verlag, 2009),11.
8. Thich Nhât Hanh *The Art of Prayer* (Weekly Magazine, 2006) Internet source https://plumvillage.org

Further to this theme, Willigis wrote in another article: "In a Zen monastery, people bow before picking up a broom and sweeping with it because it is not I who sweep, but my true being, this divine background, as this person that I am.

In a contemplation course, walking and eating continue the same contemplative presence practiced while sitting quietly. In a Benedictine monastery, whenever the hour strikes, you put down your tool or take your hands away from the computer for a minute of reflection. This is what walking in God's presence means in the Christian tradition. What is meant is: It is not I who works. This divine background works as this person and expresses itself as this person. We should have the courage to see the things in our lives as a ritual in which this divine background celebrates itself moment by moment. It can be the most ordinary things: the cup of coffee in the morning that we consciously drink; our waiting at the bus stop, or going to work could become a ritual in which we experience our innermost being."[9]

Through ongoing practice, we can gain inner stillness and fortitude. Spirituality ceases to be intellect- or emotion-based but an embodied reality that includes the entire self, one that changes how you perceive life.

Since that time at Benediktushof, I have increasingly noticed how embodied mindfulness practices and prayer are integral to life in Zen and Chan temples, ashrams, churches, and monasteries. There is an ever-growing recognition in the West of the vital importance of embodiment practices and how they can help us lead more full, rewarding, and spiritual lives.

III

In my experience with body-centered awareness practices, the Feldenkrais Method has been most helpful. This mindfulness training has immensely enriched my physical and emotional well-being and,

9. Willigis Jäger *Das Leben als Ritual* - Artikel (Holzkirchen, DE: West-Östliche Eisheit Willigis Jäger Stiftung). Internet source https://west-oestliche-weisheit.de/ueber-uns/veroeffentlichungen-willigis-jaeger)

ultimately, my spiritual life. A decade before meeting Willigis, I completed a four-year teacher training in the Feldenkrais method with Jeff Haller, Ph.D. During these years of training, significant changes opened a whole new understanding and dimension of my life. The method was a catalyst in loosening my internal entanglements and helped me move toward a new level of emotional maturity. I continue this process today using this method, my twelve-step work, and other awareness practices. And, of course, my Zen and contemplative training. I don't see these disciplines as separate; they are all part of my mystical journey.

I recall talking to Willigis about the Feldenkrais Method, which he was familiar with. He acknowledged its transformative potential and encouraged me to continue using it as awareness training and spiritual practice. In Zen Buddhism, any practice that brings about a transformative spiritual change or awakening is called a *Dharma door*. Our task is to find the most suitable practices for ourselves. As the Taoist expression states, when the shoe fits, wear it!

The Feldenkrais Method was named after its founder, Dr. Moshe Feldenkrais (1904-1984), who was an Israeli pioneer in a field now known as somatic education. He had a unique background, having been a distinguished scientist in physics and engineering and a recognized master in Judo before his full-time work with the method he created. Dr. Feldenkrais used his knowledge of Eastern martial arts and Western scientific understanding to develop a unique form of movement-based learning. His method has two applications: Awareness Through Movement, taught in group lessons, and Functional Integration when giving one-on-one lessons with a client.

This method uses movement to focus, expand awareness, and facilitate learning. It can help transform long-held patterns that adversely affect our everyday activities, behavior, and self-image. Many people use the Feldenkrais Method to move more comfortably and satisfactorily or recover from injuries and illnesses affecting their mobility. Activities, such as walking, sitting, playing a sport, writing, or working at a computer, can be improved using this method. It can also refine our abilities, such as dancing, singing, or playing an instrument. Over time, the practice has transformed my self-understanding and self-image, allowing me to drop unhelpful patterns and be more fully present and alive. At times, profound experiences of unity have occurred when working with a lesson in which body and mind merge into self-presence.

In recent years, I completed a three-year Embodied Life program with Russell and Linda Delman, two senior American Feldenkrais teachers who integrate the teachings of Moshe Feldenkrais and Zen-based meditation with communication practices, including Focusing and Guided Inquiry. The couple studied with Dr. Feldenkrais in the 1970s and were among the method's first teachers. Their program skillfully combines the core principles of Zen practice with Awareness Through Movement lessons, which allow us to inhabit our inner lives in a more open, authentic, and curious way.

The embodied practices I found in the Feldenkrais Method and Embodied Life Program are Dharma doors for me. They have enriched and complimented my spiritual life; they point the way to the great mystery, the ground of being. Such embodied awareness practices help us become fully human.

IV

As mentioned earlier in the text, I was profoundly moved by the agape ceremony at the Benediktushof community. This ceremony was called *Feier des Lebens* (celebration of life), not in the contemporary North American sense of a celebration of friends after the passing of a loved one's life. Instead, this celebration was of communal fellowship and sharing love, charity, and gratitude for the Eternal in our lives. This was an important event for Willigis, which he continued in modified form after the Vatican authorities no longer permitted him to celebrate the Eucharist officially. As for me, having grown up Catholic, I was more moved by this ceremony than any Church communion or ritual I had ever participated in.

Willigis believed that when we perform meaningful ceremonies or rituals (like the celebration of life), our psyches undergo a profound healing and integration process. He said that rituals form a bridge between the conscious and the unconscious, which enables us to find our way into our innermost being and opens us to our true nature. It is not the rituals that heal us, but the deeper, underlying life force within us becomes activated through ritual.[10]

All religious rituals and ceremonies include verbal and nonverbal prayer and sacred gestures, often archetypal. Through them, we can express our spiritual life and aspirations and build connections with others. They afford opportunities to witness, celebrate, grieve, praise, honor, and share gratitude as a community. Every ritual attempts to express some ineffable, indescribable truth in which symbolism is essential. Some rituals express a dimension that surpasses rationality, wherein the healing of a fragmented self or a fractured community can occur.

In a lecture, Willigis once said, "If we viewed our lives as a ritual celebrating the divine, the world would appear quite different. Unfortunately, this perspective isn't emphasized in religious education. Instead, we have heard far too much about sin and guilt and too little about our inherent dignity and the kingdom of God within us, which represents our true nature. Religion is not separate from our lives; it is a part of our everyday existence, where God reveals Himself and desires to dwell. So why don't we embody what we truly are—divine beings? We should see our ordinary lives as rituals in which the divine celebrates itself. If we can embrace this idea, we will live our lives with greater awareness and understanding of what Jesus meant when he said, 'The kingdom of God is within you.' Living our lives as a revelation of God applies to ourselves and all beings. The entire evolutionary process can be seen as a ritual in which God celebrates Himself. I believe this is the core meaning behind everything that happens. If we view ourselves in this light, nothing can truly harm us, as everything that happens expresses the divine source of existence. Incorporating this understanding into our daily lives will

10. Willigis Jäger *Ewige Weisheit* (München: Kösel-Verlag, 2011), 95-96.

enrich our experiences. We should celebrate our lives as rituals in which God rejoices in Himself."[11]

On a recent trip to the Haidakhandi Universal Ashram at Crestone, Colorado, my wife and I participated in the daily Fire Ceremony, a havan ritual (or homa in Sanskrit). This practice goes back more than three thousand years to the old Vedic religion of India. It is now practiced by many Hindu, Buddhist, and Jain sects today. The Fire Ceremony involves placing offerings into the fire while chanting sacred verses. The offerings are typically clarified butter and food in the form of rice, seeds, nuts, and fruit.

My beloved teacher, Haidakhandi Babaji, was fond of this ceremony and considered it a vital spiritual practice, which he said was especially important for our troubled times. He once said: "It is the fire ceremony that brings the rain that grows the grain that sustains our lives, and the smoke from the sacred fire purifies not only us but all the surrounding area, bringing peace and harmony to the surrounding cosmos." and that through this ceremony "people gain happiness and all the pleasures of life; they have beneficial thoughts and love for each other. By the smoke from the havan, the harmful germs in the atmosphere are destroyed, and the good bacteria, useful to life, grow in it. This increases the plenty and prosperity of the world."[12]

The fire ceremony is a beautiful example of an ancient ritual that is still very much alive today. A practice whose living force is shared by millions across differing religions and cultures. Other practices, like ritual bathing in holy waters, also go back to the dawn of humanity; they can be found along the banks of the Ganges or River Jordan, in baptismal rites, or in our love of the healing attributes of hot springs. Likewise,

11. Willigis Jäger *Das Leben als Ritual* - Artikel (Holzkirchen, DE: West-Östliche Eisheit Willigis Jäger Stiftung) Internet source https://west-oestliche-weisheit.de/ueber-uns/veroeffentlichungen-willigis-jaeger/

12. Pritam Rajshi *Truth, Simplicity and Love - Essential Haidakhan Babaji* (Edmonton: Roche Miette Books, 2006), 92. & Babaji on the Fire Ceremony as quoted by Ramloti at the Haidakhan Universal Ashram, Crestone, Colorado.

pilgrimages, whether going along the Camino de Santiago in Spain or to Mecca, Varanasi, a holy mountain, or some other sacred site, speak to the universality and need for a ritual life.

A spiritual ceremony can remind us that life is sacred in the grandest sense. It revitalizes the inner spiritual life and brings meaning, healing, renewal, and inspiration. The Canadian Indigenous author Richard Wagamese once said that *living in ceremony is the greatest and truest gift we can give*—a sentiment worth aspiring to.

CHAPTER 8

Aging - A Time Of Harvest

I

In his books and poems, the Irish poet John O'Donohue (1956-2008) called old age a harvest time, corresponding to when one's physical vitality diminishes.[1] That phrase, harvest time, certainly resonates with me as I migrate into my 70s. Harvest time conjures an image of reaping what one's life brought forth, a time of gratitude, thanksgiving, reflection, and pondering the legacy we leave behind. The meaning of my life takes a new urgency as my time on earth draws closer to its endpoint. I believe aging is a call to renewed spiritual practice and the harvesting of life's wisdom and insights.

In Willigis's talks and writings, Zen koans or teaching stories were often used to express spiritual insights and truths. He frequently told the following tale, which sparked my own reflections on aging and dying.

It goes as follows: "Someone asked Zen Master Ummon, 'What if the tree withers and the leaves fall?' Ummon replied, 'Perfect manifestation of the golden wind!' Meaning that if the concepts and ideas you have of things and the world fall away, what is left? The Golden Wind—the real, the essential."[2]

As Willigis explains: "In Asia, the Golden Wind also signifies the time of old age. I imagine that in this koan, two older monks sit together, and one asks the other: 'How does IT manifest itself now that we've grown old

1. John O'Donohue & John Quinn *Walking in Wonder (*Convergent / Random House, 2018)
2. Willigis Jäger *The Golden Wind or Complete your Birth! – Artikel* (Holzkirchen, DE: West-Östliche Eisheit Willigis Jäger Stiftung). Internet source https://west-oestliche-weisheit.de/ueber-uns/veroeffentlichungen-willigis-jaeger & Willigis Jäger *Der Goldene Wind* (Holzkirchen, DE: Wege-Der-Mystik, 2006), audio CD

and frail?' Is IT to be experienced in illness as an illness? In this context, Zen often speaks of Suchness, things being as they are. So IT also reveals itself as my infirmities in old age and as my incurable illness."[3]

In ancient Chinese symbolism, the wind represents the forces of vital energy known as Qi, which moves the wind. Gold, on the other hand, signifies the autumn season—a time of decline and harvest that leads into the dormancy of winter. As the above story alludes to, this also is our reality regarding aging. However, gold carries another often overlooked significance: it symbolizes preciousness and the enduring quality of long-lasting value. Similarly, we are encouraged to bring forth the hidden gifts of love, wisdom, acceptance, and perseverance as we age.

The koan speaks of a deep acceptance of how things are, just as they are, and as a way of practicing acceptance in aging. Also, this koan refers to one of the principle insights of the Buddha: that all things change and are impermanent, including this very existence! In aging, we are gifted anew and, perhaps more urgently, with the opportunity to discover what lies behind the endless flow of change in our lives. The mystics direct us to continually look past the small self (with its ego identity) to the ground of Being—the Eternal, Unborn within us, our Buddha Nature, or, as Christian mystics may say, *our life in Chris*t.

In contemplating Willigis's Golden Wind, the image of a tree emerged, which gives me solace. I picture this whole earth as a giant tree, the tree of life, in which my existence is just one leaf that appeared amongst the vastness of all its branches and leaves. Yes, this leaf will one day wither and fall; it will decompose back into the elements in the soil, but eventually, those elements will be reabsorbed back into the tree or in some other form. Thus, new life and leaves will emerge and have their days, but they, too, will fall and die only to reemerge in this ongoing cycle. Beyond this, I do not know; perhaps there are many more worlds out there with their life forms; modern science certainly thinks so. If so, this world would appear to be just one tree in an immense forest spread throughout a vast,

3. Willigis Jäger *Das Leben endet nie* (Freiburg im Breisgau: Herder Verlag, 2005), 58-59.

endless expanse of a seemingly incomprehensible universe. Such is this divine mystery we call life.

This tree of life from which I am a part is my spiritual mother, my holy mother. She gave me birth and sustains me still. Just as I have affection, love, and respect for the mother who bore me in this life, I wish to honor with an equal feeling of love, if not greater, for my divine Mother. This feeling grows with me as I journey into these elder years. And, in that love, I honor all the sacred images and names of the feminine. I do not see distinctions in how people or religion worship her, now or throughout human history. This is part of the great mystery for me, but I offer gratitude for having experienced her presence in the silence of my heart. Lao Tsu, the great Taoist sage, wrote long ago: "The spirit of the source never dies; it is called the mysterious feminine. The gates of the mysterious feminine are called the roots of heaven and earth; subtle yet everlasting, drawn from but never exhausted."[4]

Aging invites us into the harvest, into living life fully and authentically, while dying is a decisive pilgrimage to the ground of being; they both urge us to reflect on what gives us solace, comfort, and faith.

II

For some people, aging brings feelings of anxiety and fear about their current situation or, more often, about what lies ahead. These fears may be about declining health or the worries of illness that might arise; they may also be about loneliness, insecurity, loss of autonomy, or something else.

From a spiritual perspective, much of worry, fear, anxiety, and physical illness comes from a lack of spiritual nourishment. Slowly, over the years, we may have survived on little or no awareness or interest in our innermost life, having become entrapped by the ego's self-centered nature, our little self. Or perhaps some crisis occurred that broke the faith in what we once had. We have drifted into solitude and isolation, becoming disconnected

4. Lao Tsu *Tao Te Ching* - poem number 6, culled from various sources and translated by Arnie Lade

from our community or anything more significant than ourselves—the God of our understanding. Our life's purpose and meaning are lost to us; without them, we have little immunity to escape the narrow constraints of the little self, thus engendering further suffering.

Willigis said: "Disease is more than the symptoms that we have. It points us to lost connections due to stress, emotions, and fears. Healing means restoring the harmony of the whole person and healing the symptoms. This healing power is inherent and sometimes latent in every person. It is not our power but rests in our depths and wants to be awakened. It doesn't replace our usual medicine but complements it."[5]

This type of sickness relates to becoming a whole person. Mystics, like Willigis, point us toward our deepest being, which lies past our ego structure, where we can once again find healing and the organizing forces that restore wholeness. Ultimately, this involves finding renewed meaning in one's life, and a life of mindfulness, a contemplative life, gives us a pathway toward this end. This return to wholeness can, at times, alleviate and resolve illness.

When we see past the limits of the little self, true healing or wholeness emerges, and such an experience can occur bidden or unbidden amid illness, in the dying process, or, I believe, even at death. Such an awakening experience does not mean stopping the progression of disease, dying, or death from proceeding, although this sometimes occurs. Instead, it is a sign of spiritual well-being and completeness. This is the hidden gift that illness and dying can bring: a spiritual transformation when we are willing to drop our defenses, let go, and embrace the reality of the moment. Doing so can bring an entirely new openness and connection with the Eternal.

Again, I refer to Willigis: "The sufferings and uncertainties of our

5. Willigis Jäger *Das Leben endet nie* (Bielefeld: Theseus in Kamphausen Verlag, 2007), audio CD.

lives, painful and distressing, can teach us and drive us to maturity. We are far too quick to think of suffering as rejection, hostility, or punishment from life. In reality, suffering is the prerequisite for maturing and growing. No one can teach us so well as suffering. Meister Eckhart said, 'Suffering is the fastest horse to God.' Why do we suffer so much?

We have become attached to how things were or are supposed to be. The sufferings and pains of our lives are the path; experience the pain you can't escape. Don't experience it fatalistically and masochistically; attend to it with the certainty that it brings something new... when fear comes, accept it and don't fight it. Stay present in the moment. However, it may present itself! The more practice we have in letting go and accepting, the more bearable the present moment becomes... We can lament suffering or try to use it to grow and mature. The first prerequisite for this is acceptance. I accept the situation that I cannot change at the moment. Suffering will transform us. And real joy comes from letting go of ultimately untenable positions—whoever can let go gains! Suffering is the price of maturity and wisdom."[6]

Of course, illness and disease may require the right medicine in a suitable form, whether through drugs, psychotherapy, surgery, or some other natural means. However, this does not negate the need to heal any lingering spiritual suffering we may harbor. The first step is fully accepting one's situation and then moving forward to take whatever action is necessary and possible.

As a longtime acupuncturist, I have seen many clients restore their inner lives to balance and resolve diseases. In acupuncture, this is done by accessing and communicating with those deeper impulses of body, mind, and spirit. The treatment method involves working with the Qi, the life force communicating with and mediating between the body, mind, and spirit. Deep listening and compassionate speech also form intimate aspects of helping someone to return to wholeness, while love is the

6. Willigis Jäger *Freude trotz Leid - Der Großte Meister des Lebens* Internet source: www.west-oestliche-weisheit.de/ueber-uns/veroeffentlichungen-willigis-jaeger

resonance of the ground of being itself. True healing by a practitioner is the art of accompanying someone towards the source of their being, to whatever extent they can and choose to go.

III

In 2013, Willigis wrote a paper on aging and dying shortly after his birthday, when he was already deep into his aging process. From my perspective, it was a process he faced with dignity, and he used his experiences to help others. Willigis's writing, when I first read it, deeply moved me, and I quickly translated it to give to friends, and they, too, appreciated his insights. I showed Willigis my translation a few months later that year at Benediktushof, which he permitted me to publish.[7]

I invite you to read and then, after some time, reread this letter as a contemplative reflection. As a senior, you can also share this writing with a group for a contemplative discussion. A contemplative discussion or dialogue means mindfully reading a text, followed by a reflective conversation in which participants share and listen to each other with respect.

> *Dear Companions on the Way,*
>
> I recently celebrated my 88th birthday. Thank you all for your well wishes. I wish you, too, could reach this age, if not more.
>
> Again and again, the question of aging has been asked of me. What is the situation with aging? We live in a culture where being young is glorified while aging receives little support and understanding. We feel obligated to stay young. But human life is a perpetual becoming. This applies even as the bodily forces subside and hearing and sight are diminished. Just then, the meaning of life is renewed decisively. Living through this extreme situation

7. Willigis Jäger's article was translated by Arnie Lade with permission & published in Greenspirit News, 2013.

can lead to an unprecedented encounter with oneself and a whole new openness to the meaning of life.

How can we respond positively to aging?

1. Accept the aging process and say YES to these life changes. Then, we can discover new opportunities that only ripe old age can offer, and then this time of life will not be viewed as a passive decline but rather as the fulfillment of human existence.

2. Old age is a time of increased turning toward the ground of being, our true life. It gives us a chance to be wise. We were locked into the care and responsibility of family and livelihood for a long time. In old age, we can slowly distance ourselves from things and gain a new perspective on love, the world, and people. Wisdom cannot be learned from books but from gradual growth and maturation.

3. The interest in and enjoyment of beautiful things, music, literature, and religion grows. Psychology tells us that people do not even live to half their physical and mental capacity. Many rooms in the house of the soul are sealed and never opened. Some older people suddenly discover new opportunities and energy sources they had no idea they had until now. Our task is to use this latent potential. It's never too late to discover unexplored areas of our personality and develop them. Our life is timeless. Luther said, "If I knew that that world would end tomorrow, I would still plant my apple tree today."

4. Meeting Anxiety. First, we need to distinguish between knowable fears and anxiety. These fears refer to something specific, such as illness, marriage/partnership problems, injuries, slander, and so forth. At the same time, anxiety is usually more vague and unspecific, a mood or feeling without any specific object. This anxiety is often what torments older people. It threatens the personality and can paralyze and

destroy. Anxiety hinders us from letting go of that which we cherish and cling to. But anxiety and the feeling of threat that may arise can also have a beneficial effect in that it moves us to realize and accept our limitations. Thus, through anxiety, a wholesome experience of the reality of our own mortality can come about. Anxiety can then be a saving experience.

5. Don't let worries depress you. A missionary asked a Japanese man what led him to become a Christian. Without hesitation, he replied, "Do not worry about your life, what you will eat or drink; or about your body, what you will wear." (Mathew 6:25) And he continued, "During my life, I had many worries about my health, my children, the future, about growing old. I never felt right or happy, but then I read that passage from the Sermon on the Mount about the providence of God who takes care of the birds in the air and the lilies in the field. After that, I felt liberated from all my anxieties and fears."

6. Accept suffering. The crucial task in old age is and remains (as in life) to end suffering. In the sufferings of old age, man experiences the whole meaning of the words of Jesus, "Amen, I tell you: unless a kernel of wheat falls to the ground and dies, it remains alone. But if it dies, it produces much Fruit." (John 12:24) One then understands another saying of Jesus, which he once spoke to Peter, "Amen, I tell you, when you were younger you dressed yourself and went where you wanted; but when you are old you will stretch out your hands, and someone else will dress you and lead you where you do not want to go." (John 21:18)

7. Mourning. The older you get, the more often you must take leave of loved ones. We must accept this loss. Letting go is one of the most challenging tasks of our lives and yet one of the most important. All we hold too tightly is deadly for us. If we hold our breath, we suffocate. Whoever holds on prevents themself from growing and maturing. Even with a loved one,

we should not try to hold on. Otherwise, we stop them from completion. We must mourn. From this grief comes gratitude for our time together and hope for another meeting.

8. Religious dimension of aging. "Everything has its own time" (Ecclesiastes 3). Aging gives us the opportunity for religious maturity. As our physical forces decrease, we can experience the divine ground of being becoming the fundamental aspect of life. In our impotence and weakness, the timeless ground of being, our true nature, is perfected. When we cannot do anything more than accept others' loving-kindness, the timeless ground of being awaits us.

9. Dying, to live. In this modern age, mortality and death are hidden and difficult to accept. For physicians, death is too often viewed as a final breakdown that we must struggle against. Only our limited ego-consciousness sets us apart from the universal, timeless life. So, how can we alleviate the fear of death? Only when we are willing to die can we say Yes to life. We know that our time on earth is very short. But if we realize that our true nature knows no time, we understand life and death quite differently. All suffering and fear come from the fact that we do not know who we really are. This mortal life, here and now, expresses eternal life. We can call it God's Life, for God is the name of this ground of being from which everything arises.

Death is the mystical crossing—a return to the source of Being. The true mystic does not separate between this world and the hereafter. What we call this world is but a limited reality that we experience with our mind and senses.

CHAPTER 9

Reflections On Death and Dying

I

In Willigis's writings and talks, the topic of death and dying is often addressed. At first, I wondered if this might be due to his own advancing years. That is until I read the following by Brother David Steindl-Rast, a fellow Benedictine, which helped me understand why this topic was of such significance for Willigis. Steindl-Rast writes: "In the rule of St. Benedict, the *momenta mori* has always been important because one of what St. Benedict calls 'the tools of good works,' meaning the basic approach to the daily life of the monastery is to have death at all times before one's eyes. When I first came across the Benedictine Rule and tradition, it was one of the key sentences that impressed and attracted me very much. It challenged me to incorporate the awareness of death into my daily living, for that is what it really amounts to. It isn't primarily a practice of thinking of one's last hour or of death as a physical phenomenon; it is a seeing of every moment of life against the horizon of death and a challenge to incorporate that awareness of dying into every moment so as to become more fully alive."[1]

Willigis's frequent reflections and discussions about death stem from a deeply personal experience. He shared in his writings and talks that a near-death incident significantly altered his perspective on life. This occurred when a medication caused his heart to stop for a period. At that moment, he felt like he was on the verge of dying and entered into an overwhelming silence and profound emptiness. There was no sense of self, only love, total acceptance, and a feeling of oneness, an experience

1. David Steindl-Rast *Learning to Die* (article in Parabola Magazine, February 29, 2016 edition) Internet source: https://parabola.org

that lasted two days. Since that time, Willigis said the fear of death had left him, and he realized one fundamental truth: life is eternal. [2]

He wrote, "When I transcended the boundaries of the self, I realized that dying is an illusion. I stood at the threshold, prepared to move forward; it felt less like an ending and more like an invitation into a more profound, blissful reality. An incredible silence enveloped me. I could describe it as emptiness, but this emptiness had a quality that beckoned me to come closer. However, my time to depart had not yet arrived. It became clear that my desire to cross over was futile; one must be called. And that all reality simply exists, for in that moment, there was no division, no opposition—just unity.

What remained was the certainty that I was not what I once believed I was. Everything originates from the essence we call God, and nothing can be separated from it. I also understood that even what we label as evil is not separate; it is merely a lack of awareness. I felt a profound reverence for others and a sacred respect for myself, for my dignity, and also for the dignity of those who commit terrible acts—terrorists and slave drivers alike. Nothing was exempt. Every being is a radiant spiritual center. When the outer shell falls away, a person discovers their true origins and realizes they have never been anywhere else."[3]

I often heard Willigis say, more or less, these exact words: "After birth, death is the most important event in our lives—it completes our birth. When we die, it's not that we submit to death; rather, we submit to the progression of life, which knows no lingering. We don't lose something when we die; we gain something; we regain the entire universe hidden behind our ego. We win God back completely, undisguised of the ego.

2. Willigis Jäger Über Die Liebe (München: Kösel-Verlag, 2011), 132-133. & *Es Gibt Keinen Tod* (Holzkirchen, DE: Wege-Der-Mystik, 2006), audio CD. & Willigis Jäger *Das Leben endet nie* (Bielefeld: Theseus in Kamphausen Verlag, 2007).

3. Willigis Jäger *Es Gibt Keinen Tod* – Artikel (Holzkirchen, DE: West-Östliche Eisheit Willigis Jäger Stiftung). Internet source https://west-oestliche-weisheit.de/ueber-uns/veroeffentlichungen-willigis-jaeger

Nothing already separates us from life; only our ego experiences itself as separate from life."[4]

From a mystical perspective, including Zen teachings, life and death are not opposites but two ends of the same life process. This spiritual view transcends the concepts of birth and death, the afterlife, or rebirth; it focuses instead on transcendence in this life. Thus, the fundamental task is to be fully human, live our lives accordingly, and recognize that we are a form of the Unborn, the Eternal. When we say YES to this form, we can truly live life as an act of worship and celebration.

For me, the finality of death, of this physical form, challenges me to be fully present here and now and strive to live to my potential. Ultimately, when death arrives, my task will be to let go into this great mystery, which is beyond my rational comprehension. But I know, in the words of my Zen teacher, Rev. Master Meiten: "If death weren't natural, it wouldn't be." And yes, of course, fear and anxiety most probably will arise, for I understand that my little self, with its inherent self-centeredness, doesn't want to perish and disappear. It's natural to feel anxiety and fear when the physical body's survival is being questioned. My task will be to let go, let go, and let go some more! And that, all my letting go, little and big, over the years, in both contemplative practice and daily life, is also preparation for the ultimate letting go in dying and death. It's a spiritual practice, and remembering this helps me live better.

Willigis wrote: "Our real problem is not dying but our attachment to a particular form, this shape we have now. Each form has its unmistakable meaning. As I am, I am the manifestation of reality's goodness. My real task is to be human, to be human with all the potential that we are given. And Rumi sings enthusiastically: 'Before there were gardens, vines or grapes in this world, our soul was already drunk with the wine of immortality.' And again, Eckhart preaches: 'When I go back into God. When I go into the ground, into the soil, into the stream, and the source of divinity, no one

4. Willigis Jäger *Über den Tod Hinaus* (article in Zeitschrift Wege, 2006 edition). Internet source https://west-oestliche-weisheit.de/ueber-uns/veroeffentlichungen-willigis-jaeger

will ask me where I come from or where I have been. Nobody missed me there.' And he continues: 'And therefore I am unborn, and that is why I can never die. Because of my unbornness, I have been eternal and am now and will remain eternal. What I am by my birth will die and come to nothing, for it is temporary."[5]

II

In *Death: The Final Stage of Growth*, Elisabeth Kübler-Ross (1926-2004), a prominent American psychiatrist and eminent authority on death and dying, emphasized in her teachings the importance of accepting the finiteness of life. She observes that we can find inner strength and motivation to live fully and authentically when we deeply acknowledge our limited time on earth. In contrast, living as if we will never die can lead to neglecting the preciousness of the present moment, and all too often, we can end up postponing necessary actions and, ultimately, living empty and purposeless lives. Kübler-Ross encouraged living each day as if it were our last, embracing growth and reaching out to others. She also highlighted the significance of practicing life with compassion, love, courage, patience, hope, and faith. She emphasized that "Death is the final stage of growth in this life. There is no total death. Only the body dies. The self or spirit, or whatever you wish to label it, is eternal."[6]

I once asked Willigis, in a private interview during a retreat, what he believed happens after death—in rebirth, an afterlife, or what. He answered that he didn't believe in either resurrection or reincarnation, and suddenly he stood up, spread out his hands to shoulder height, and exclaimed that he was 'ready to let go completely when the time came, and merge back with everything, into the ground of being—the Eternal.' But then he said: 'But you can believe what you want; it doesn't matter what you believe, it's not the essential part.' I understood it's more consequential

5. Willigis Jäger *Es Gibt Keinen Tod* - Artikel (Holzkirchen, DE: West-Östliche Eisheit Willigis Jäger Stiftung) Internet source https://west-oestliche-weisheit.de/ueber-uns/veroeffentlichungen-willigis-jaeger/

6. Elisabeth Kübler-Ross *Death The Final Stage of Growth* (New York: Prentice-Hall, 1975), 164-166.

how I live, practice, and love here and now than what I believe; my ideas, images, and ideals of what happens are not what counts, for the mystery of death is beyond understanding. Today, I recognize that fully living and loving matters most and that saying yes to life is also saying yes to its completion.

Willigis writes, "All spiritual paths teach us to let go so that our true immortal self can shine through. They teach us that saying YES to death is the gateway to life. We are not talking about a denial of death as a way of seeking to live forever, but rather, a transcendence of birth and death. We look upon ourselves as mortal because we lose this outer form, but our true being knows neither birth nor death. We put it incorrectly when we say: 'I was born,' in reality, we should say: 'My essence was born in the 'I' you see before you.' The most essential part of a human being is never born and never dies. We fear death because we identify so closely with our ego. Our ego always seeks permanence. Mysticism aims to awaken us to our true nature, free of birth and death. It teaches us not to flee either death or birth, but rather to transcend both."[7]

III

A few years ago, I picked up a book entitled *A Year to Live: How to Live This Year as If It Were Your Last* [8], written by Stephen Levine (1937-2016). It's an intriguing book written by the noted American author and teacher of the art of living and dying mindfully. As the title suggests, one of the exercises in the book is to reflect on what would be most vital to you if you knew you had a terminal illness and only a year left to live.

That summer, I pondered and journaled on this question while vacationing on a small island in the Salish Sea, a place free of life's usual distractions and busyness. Out of my journalling, I made a short list of what would become my spiritual intention and practice for the

7. Willigis Jäger *Timeless Eternal Wisdom* translated by Marie-André Horsthemke (Dublin: Logos Publications, 2014), 61.

8. Steven Levine *A Year to Live: How to Live This Year as If It Were Your Last* (New York: Harmony Books, 1998)

following twelve months. My discernment focused on a recommitment to sharing love and gratitude, renewing connections and healing strained relationships, and, most importantly, cultivating my connection to the ground of being. I put aside my previous fantasies and notions of my future, like travel plans, imaginary holidays, various projects, consumer purchases, etc.

I benefited so much from the above exercise of a year left to live that I also journaled a five-year version. What would be essential if I had just five years to live? This could guide me further, assuming that living another five years was probable. This, too, proved helpful in setting me on a course to live more wholeheartedly and with a renewed contemplative commitment. It helped reaffirm a new perspective in which love became the principal foundation of how I wanted to live life, and that this aspiration would be love in its most inclusive form: compassion and agape, and keeping faith and fidelity with my ground of being my true nature.

As Willigis and other mystics remind us, what we hold in our hands at the end of our lives is not our achievements and works but rather how much we have loved.

IV

Since doing this exercise of writing out my intentions and living them to the best of my abilities, my older brother Al passed away after many years of living with Parkinson's Disease. I found this to be a vulnerable feeling, knowing that I, too, was getting ever closer to death. My parents had died many years before, and my brother's death brought me *one notch closer to the top of the totem pole*—that there are not too many left ahead of me in our family lineage, let alone the increasing number of friends who have already departed.

Of course, losing my brother brought up feelings of grief: a person who shared my history, childhood, and our common memories. Al had witnessed the arch of my life's journey as I had his. Grief is utterly natural and okay, although it's challenging to endure. It's a sign you felt something for that person! Thankfully, the end of his life was a blessed one where his loving family surrounded him. May we all be so fortunate!

In the movie Shadowlands, the biographical drama about the relationship between the author C.S. Lewis and his American wife, Lewis says after his wife died in his deep grief and suffering: "The pain I feel now is the happiness I had before. That's the deal."[9] Grief reminds us how deeply touched we have been by the one who has left us and now entered an unseen existence, the ever-present Eternal.

When we recognize that grief is an aspect of love that appeared in the form of one we loved, who has now passed beyond our time into death, grief can be seen in its proper perspective. Love will always exist; it was and remains in our hearts. Grief after loss calls us to open our hearts and allow it to cleanse us so we can love more fully.

Grief becomes unbearable when we hold it tight. Mindfulness and spiritual training teach us to let feelings flow through us like a river, letting them go. And not to fear their presence, for they will pass like water through a river. Should it remain blocked or submerged, it can bring about spiritual and physical illness. In my life, I have witnessed people who had not healed from their grief. As a result, they became ill, and in some cases, it broke their hearts, and they died under its unbearable strain.

Through spiritual practice, we can learn to bear all our feelings, even those that seem unbearable, intolerable, or unjust. We can practice with one feeling at a time, listening to it, accepting and expressing it, and being open to its hidden messages. Our feelings will surely diminish with practice, and eventually, we will be released from their grip.

9. *Shadowlands* (Film, 1993) - A British biographical drama film about the relationship between academic C. S. Lewis and American poet Joy Davidman, her death from cancer, and how this challenged his Christianity; directed by Richard Attenborough with a screenplay by William Nicholson.

A loved one's death can give us, those who remain here, a renewed outlook on our lives and the days ahead. That is, once we pass through our grief. My friend Judi Trost wrote the following moving poem after the loss of her sister:

when death comes,
the heart made tender
by the leaving,
bringing more love
to the living

when death comes,
a reminder of the finite
in the infinite.

live now, gently held
in the Eternal,
do not wait for
when death comes [10]

V

Willigis lived a well-lived life, one that led him to the ground of being—the Eternal. He inspired me personally, and I know he didn't want anyone to try to emulate him but to walk their own path. I imagine Willigis saying to me, "Fully be Arnie as Arnie, here and now!"

I found the following poem by Willigis very moving, in which he expresses gratitude for the life he had lived. It was released after he died in 2020, but it was written in 2015, Willigis having requested that the poem not be published until after his death.

10. Poem by Judi Trost, published with permission.

I give thanks,
for being allowed to exist
in this body
at this time
at this place
through the times I've lived
for all my experiences and encounters,
for knowing myself
for all those who accompanied me along the way,
as well as those who had difficulty with me
and I thank everyone with whom
I'm connected with in love.
The Source has no distinctions,
that which we call God,
unites us and all forms in love. [11]

11. Alexander Poraj-Zakiej *Das Willigis Jahrhundert* (Holzkirchen, DE: West-Östliche Eisheit Willigis Jäger Stiftung 2020), 211.

CHAPTER 10

Walking Life's Labyrinth

I

About twelve years ago, I spent a month on a work-study program at Benediktushof. Part of my job was caring for the outdoor labyrinth in the open field behind the retreat center's main buildings. I would hand-weed the entire labyrinth and then patiently cut the grass along its raised bed surface. The total diameter of the circular labyrinth was about fifteen meters. Over time, I became intimately familiar with it by caring for it and walking its path in contemplative silence.

Walking the labyrinth engages one's entire being and symbolizes the mystical, spiritual path. As I entered the labyrinth, a narrow footpath led me along a winding circular route that repeatedly doubled back on itself. At times along the way, I seemed to come close to its center, and at other times, I found myself on its outer edges, unsure of how far I'd come. But I followed the path one footstep after the other, wanting to stay mindfully present. When I reached the midpoint at the labyrinth's center, I paused to recollect, contemplate, and give thanks. Then, I pivoted, turned around, and walked back through its circuitous route to where I began, refreshed and revitalized. Each time I walked the labyrinth that summer, it offered a fresh experience, much like my daily meditation practice, wherein nothing dramatic usually occurs, yet there are subtle changes.

Walking the labyrinth is an ancient practice that is as alive today as it was in the past. There's probably a labyrinth somewhere close to you. Even here, where I write these pages on a small island off Canada's West Coast, there is a labyrinth in the forest surrounded by old Douglas fir trees. People come to walk it regularly, just as they do in many places worldwide. I have walked on beautifully paved labyrinth paths made of colored marble slates and ones on dry earth with paths marked by simple stones. They can be found in backyard gardens and magnificent cathedrals; all kinds of labyrinths exist.

The origins of the labyrinth are unknown, but the best-known historical ones are those on the island of Crete, in the Mediterranean Sea, from around 500 BC. They are associated with classical Greece and are mentioned in the Minotaur story. However, unlike the maze-like labyrinth in the Minotaur story, which has choices and dead ends, the modern labyrinth has only a single path in and out to its center, despite all its twists and turns.

Today, walking the labyrinth is known as a spiritual, contemplative practice. It represents the spiritual path of self-transformation, which is neither linear nor without difficulties, including times of loneliness, confusion, frustrations, doubts, inner wastelands, and the demise and death of the ego. The spiritual and mystical path can be a dramatic process at times, one that takes us to the edges and past our ego toward our actual being. We move from the little self to the larger self, the ground of our being.

For the noted psychologist Carl Jung, the labyrinth symbolized the process of individuation, becoming a whole person (which is another way of saying the mystical journey.) He writes: "... the right way to wholeness is made up, unfortunately, of fateful detours and wrong turnings."[1]

Willigis writes: "The labyrinth is a way of life. You walk through the narrow entrance. The center beckons you. Suddenly, there were bends and turns and a tangle of corridors. Do they lead to the middle? Don't they lead away from the goal? Twisting and turning, is that still the direction? Since the middle is very close, why does the path now lead outwards? Doubts arise—is this the right way? Isn't that the beginning again? Haven't we been here before? Don't give up or get stuck because only those who go on will reach their destination. Detours are times of purification, transformation, and maturation. Courage and perseverance

1. Carl Gustav Jung, C.G. *The Collected Works of C. G. Jung Vol. 12 - Psychology and Alchemy* (Princeton, NJ: Princeton University Press, 1980), Sec. 1, 4.

are the thread that leads you through bright and dark days. The middle is certain for you, the big goal... if you stay on the path."[2]

II

As we walk this spiritual path, there can be disorientation and uncertainty, just like in a labyrinth or, worse, a perplexing maze. The encouragement and guidance from someone who can help us avoid losing sight of the way can be most beneficial. You might be best served by finding a trusted guide before starting the journey to prevent unnecessary difficulty. Spiritual direction from a teacher or spiritual friend is sometimes vital, if not essential.

Willigis often gave the analogy of a teacher being like a mountain guide who accompanies and helps a person climb to the destination, to the top, and back down again. The guide knows the pitfalls and dead-ends, when the conditions are ripe to ascend, when to stay put or even back off, and to lend a hand, encourage, and warn us of dangers. Before climbing together, it's good to have confidence in your guide and to know them well enough to trust them. Willigis reminds us that a guide can only take you as far as they have gone along themselves and over the terrain they know best. But their role is crucial in helping us face our difficulties and grow. Ultimately, we have to transverse it with our own two feet.

The influential 20th-century German psychologist and Zen teacher Karlfried Dürckheim once commented that a true spiritual friend does not encourage the old, historic self to survive but inspires us to continue along our path despite challenging times. Dürckheim championed spiritual daring, a quality that demands courage to face our difficulties head-on, stating that "when a person on their spiritual path encounters difficulties, they are best advised not to take refuge with a friend who only offers comfort and suggests avoiding one's troubles, thereby maintaining the status quo of the false self. Instead, it would be better to seek someone who will steadfastly and continually help them bravely face and move

2. Willigis Jäger & Beatrice Grimm *Der Himmel in Dir* (München: Kösel-Verlag, 2009), 176.

through their difficulties, using such struggles to deepen their spiritual practice. In doing so, the false self becomes gradually dismantled, allowing the true self to come forth." [3]

For teachers like Willigis and Dürckheim, spiritual practice aims not to develop an attitude that protects us from being disturbed by life but rather to become resilient and learn from life's difficulties, troubles, and hardships. In doing so, we become open to inner transformation. We learn to accept ourselves and our lives, including all that arises within our thoughts, feelings, and behaviors. In this way, we slowly, over time, dismantle the delusions of the false self and learn to contact the true self, and the possibilities of a new life become open.

Along the spiritual path, we need such friends, teachers, and mentors who can unreservedly reflect their perspective of our journey. Ideally, they will become our trusted companions, accompanying us as we journey together. In the early texts of Buddhism, such a person is called a *Kalyanamitra*, or spiritual friend. Kalyana means "virtuous, good, true, or beneficial," and Mitra is the root word for kindness. Such a person with these qualities is a profound blessing in our lives and for awakening our true selves.

III

In my life, I have been blessed to have had three such spiritual guides who have accompanied me at various times along the way. The first was Haidakhan Babaji, whom I met in India during the early 1980s. Despite being with him for a short time, I still consider him my beloved teacher. Babaji taught the Eternal Dharma, emphasizing the principles of truth, simplicity, and love. Babaji was free of religious and cultural limitations; even though he was embedded in Hindu culture and religion, he was a great teacher whose teachings went beyond creeds. Babaji is a personification of what it means to be truly human, in communion with the Eternal.

3. Karlfried Dürckheim *Der Alltag als Übung* (Bern: Verlag Hans Huber, 1966), 100-101.

My second teacher was the Reverend Master Meiten, a Zen Buddhist dharma teacher in the Order of Buddhist Contemplatives who lived in our hometown. My wife and I studied with her and came to know her quite well. We immediately connected with her at our first meeting and liked her openness to different traditions. Rev. Meiten had once lived and taught at the Yasodhara Ashram, a Yoga center in our province.

Rev. Meiten helped us through a challenging period of life, individually and as a couple and family. She inspired me to commit more fully to my spiritual journey and to heal myself and my relationships. She had been a professor of psychology before entering the monastery, and this, with her Buddhist monastic training, gave her a remarkable ability to listen, discern the roots of suffering, and give spiritual direction. Her various writings were compiled into one recent volume: *Coming Home: Taking Refuge Within*. It is an excellent resource on spiritual and Buddhist practice in the nitty-gritty of every day.[4]

We stayed with Rev. Meiten until she passed away, and we continue to participate in the local Sangha (spiritual community) she started and keep in touch with other monks in her Order. A couple of years ago, I attended the Precepts ceremony at the Mount Shasta Buddhist Abbey to renew and deepen my commitment to the Precepts I first took as a young man. It was a wonderful week studying Buddhist Precepts and their underlying spiritual principles. The week also included a series of ceremonial reenactments, symbolic of their profound meaning and purpose in one's life. Rev. Meiten would have been pleased; I certainly was!

My third great teacher is Willigis, whom I write about in this book. I had a very profound connection with him, not in a personal sense, but of spiritual resonance; call it karmic, if you will. There was an almost immediate and intuitive knowing from my first meeting that he would be a significant mentor for me. And that he knew me in a way that unlocked my koans and quickened my path to the ground of being. I

4. Meiten McGuire *Coming Home: Taking Refuge Within* (Victoria, BC: Vancouver Island Zen Sangha, 2022)

first encountered Willigis's writings in a book called *Searching for the Meaning of Life*, one of his few books translated into English. I found it by chance in my local used bookstore. Rev. Meiten encouraged me to follow my compelling inner urge to study with Willigis in Germany, and for that, I am grateful.

All three teachers had very different personalities, cultural backgrounds, languages, teaching styles, and, to some extent, approaches to spiritual life. However, each of their lives exemplified the mystical path of awakening, and each, in their ways, helped others to follow theirs. Another critical point I can attest to is that they wholeheartedly accepted and honored all authentic spiritual paths. This is an essential characteristic of a mature teacher and a good criterion in choosing a spiritual friend and teacher—someone who is open and accepting of all paths and accepts you for who you are, not on some religious or cultural doctrine that discriminates by race, gender, nationality or belief.

When choosing a teacher, Willigis gave us this advice: "I am more in favor of the old saying: Every teacher has the students he deserves, and every student has the teacher he deserves. In the end, the teacher's personality and character determine who will come to them. Only those teachers whose path is attractive and practicable and who have the trust of their students should be considered. A relationship of trust must exist between student and teacher on a spiritual path. If that is not the case, the two should mutually agree to go separate ways."[5]

Willigis counseled that spiritual direction involved helping individuals look behind their ego structure. Such guidance encourages focusing on inner transformation rather than making external changes, especially at the beginning of the spiritual journey. For Willigis, spiritual growth and transformation occur from the inside out. And as the ego structure is clarified, we can learn to perceive what lies behind its superficial facade—the true self. He believed that having a loving companion who understands

5. Willigis Jäger Willigis Jäger *Mysticism for Modern Times* (Liguori, Missouri: Liguori-Triumph, 2006), 38-39.

this process can significantly contribute to one's spiritual experience. For many, feeling accepted and loved just as they are by a trusted companion is an affirming gift and a deeply meaningful experience.[6]

Although these three great teachers have passed away, they remain a source of refuge and inspiration for me, and I carry their love, companionship, and blessings in my heart.

Ultimately, there can be no imitation of others along the way, of teachers, spiritual friends, or those we might venerate; ultimately, we must become spiritual adults. In the words of Matsuo Bashō, a famous 17th-century Haiku poet and Zen Buddhist, he advises: *do not follow in the footsteps of the ancients; instead, seek what they sought.*[7] Yes, our teachers and mentors can show us the way, but we must do the walking. Moreover, no one can awaken you, for it is in you already. The ground of being, the true self, is always there; it only needs to be uncovered.

IV

Once, I had an experience that illustrates the help a teacher can offer in a spiritual crisis. It happened to me about ten years ago following an emergency gallbladder surgery.

On the second day after surgery, in the morning, my mind was increasingly becoming unreliable, subjected to fragmented thoughts, along with hypersensitivity to all sensations and a rapidly decreasing sense of self. There was also great emotional fragility, vulnerability, and feeling porous to everything around me. It was something like coming down from an LSD trip but exaggerated many times over. All the while, fear and anxiety grew as the sense of losing *my* 'self' intensified, which was accompanied by a lack of any agency to control what was occurring. Thoughts arose that perhaps I was experiencing a kind of dying or death process—the little self was panicking!

6. Willigis Jäger *Über Die Liebe* (München: Kösel-Verlag, 2011), 19.

7. Matsuo Bashō quote - *Collaborative Reference Database* Internet Source: https://crd.ndl.go.jp/reference (quote: 古人の跡をもと めず、古人の求たる所を. もとめよ)

The first night at home, sleeping, was the most challenging, and if it hadn't been for my wife Diane's help, I don't know how I would have made it through the night. I could hardly sink into sleep without an involuntarily choking sensation occurring. Diane stayed with me and gave me some Somato-Experiencing tools for trauma that I used as I lay in bed. And the sleep I did get (perhaps an hour or two) was of a light, nightmarish, dream-filled quality.

By the following morning, I felt more tired and worn out; my nervous system was even more fragile. I was very emotional. I was at wit's end, barely hanging on. My mind was very much troubled. In the afternoon, I called Reverend Master Meiten, our Zen Buddhist teacher. I tried to describe what was happening, and after listening, she said: "Is awareness still there?" I replied, "Yes." Rev. Meiten said, "Stay with that." She then gave me some clear and reassuring advice: no matter how difficult and disorientating the experience was, I needed to stay with awareness; that *awareness was the key* and the foundation for spiritual practice. I understood this to mean that simply abiding in awareness, continuing to let everything else go, and letting things take their course was the path of freedom from my suffering. My fear and uncertainty, perceived inability to function, and the disorientation of losing my sense of self, as distressing as it may be, were all aspects of the limited, historic little self, and that awareness itself was the true pathfinding freedom. Most importantly, this awareness was connected to the eternal Unborn within. I don't know all the exact words Rev. Meiten spoke that day, but much weight was lifted from my struggles.

My dreams changed that second night at home; they became more emotional, and lots of crying and feelings of grief and sorrow were in them. However, my sleep was a little deeper - mostly, I floated in the dream state, not sinking too far into a deep sleep. But, right toward the morning, I had an integrative dream. In the dream, Willigis came to me and said: "You were given this experience to know that in this reality, including oneself, all things arise and fall away; nothing is permanent. You have been shown a deeper reality, which is awareness itself, and a path that leads directly to the ground of being, the source of our true self."

Interestingly, this dream was in German, and I slowly translated it back to English when I awoke!

The following day, I was much more peaceful and rested. Between the reassuring conversation with Rev. Meiten and the healing dream with Willigis, I started to settle down. I felt relaxed and allowed the whole process of healing and restoration of my nervous system to unfold. I practiced just staying with the awareness and letting go. My heart was opening to trust and gratitude more and more. I felt such love and peace and a new depth of understanding.

V

Today, I choose to spend more time with spiritual friends and seek their counsel whenever needed. I also attend retreats with various groups, specifically but not exclusively within the Zen tradition, in which I feel most at home. Willigis advised me to attend one or two retreats a year and study with other teachers. I have found gaining perspective through different teachings helpful, but I also need to discern what works for me.

I also need community, for that is where my spiritual growth meets the timeless test of daily reality. My interactions reflect where I am in the journey to becoming a whole, spiritually upright person. We can support and help each other in a community of friends and companions who walk the path alongside us. In the community, we can experience the riches of belonging, love, and acceptance. Nevertheless, we must also be vigilant so that the historic, conditioned self does not project its judgments, aversions, and desires onto others. We must practice our spiritual precepts and maintain sound ethical behaviors to avoid the many pitfalls in our interactions with others. Unfortunately, we often hear teachers and students who have succumbed to self-centeredness and self-satisfying behaviors—that is not the path!

I endeavor to practice warm-hearted mindfulness in all my relationships. I find it helpful to frequently reflect on my behaviors, speech, and actions when being with others, especially those closest to me, who seem to bear the brunt of my little self (with all its afflictions, quirks, and anxieties). I also use daily reflections, such as: How have I treated my family, friends, and strangers today? Have I been present in life's comings and goings? Have I been open and honest with myself or others? Have I made amends for any harm done? How could I have done better in a situation that bothered me? And most importantly, how much have I loved and shown kindness and compassion?

Willigis once said: "Whoever enters this experience learns unity, connection, and love. This love leads to community, a fellowship with anyone and everyone. This shows itself as the meaning of our humanity. This experience leads back to our everyday lives. It allows us to understand life differently and explains the meaning of our short lifetime in this timeless universe."[8]

Recently, we started a meditation group that meets in our home; it's a small community of friends that have come together to share in the nourishment of silently sitting and walking together in meditation. As part of our meetings, we read spiritual literature or poems, followed by a contemplative dialogue after meditation. Our conversation is open-hearted, deep listening to ourselves and each other, which allows us to discern our inner voices of wisdom. To be amongst friends in this way is most intimate and unique. Nothing needs to be said at times, for those are reflective moments as significant as when words do surface.

Most importantly, what arises from our collective presence is loving-kindness. We can gain much nourishment in such fellowship, inspire each other, and become the best versions of our authentic selves.

Meister Eckhart, the great Dominican mystic, once said: "The most important hour is always the present moment, the most important person is always the one who is facing you right now, and the most necessary work is always love."[9]

8. Alexander Poraj-Zakiej *Das Willigis Jahrhundert* (Holzkirchen, DE: West-Östliche Eisheit Willigis Jäger Stiftung 2020), 209.

9. Maria Kolek Braun *Im Gespräch Sein* (Holzkirchen, DE: Benediktushof Magazin - Online-Artikel) Internet source: https://www.benediktushof-holzkirchen.de/im-gespraech-sein/

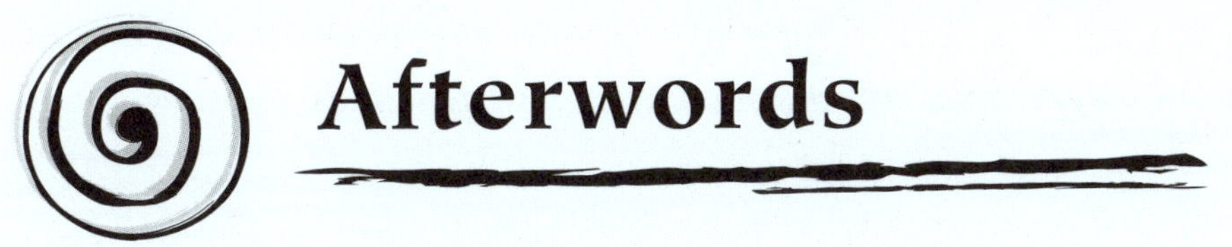

Afterwords

A quarter century ago, Willigis wrote, "Fundamental transformation of the world will never be achieved by a new social system, but only through the transformation of the individual. We always cry for the great surgeon to come and perform the crucial operation. But those who want to change the world will not rely on specialists. Only those who leave behind the routines of society—overcoming greed, the mania for possessions, and the hunger for power—will ever change anything."[1]

Humanity's history has undoubtedly shown us that our relationship with the world will not fundamentally change through politics, revolution, or wars but through individual self-transformation, one that leads us out of the ego tunnel. Mystics, like Willigis, warn us that inner transformation must proceed ahead of outer change; otherwise, it cannot endure, for it will be subsumed by the same narrow self-centeredness that has brought us to this critical juncture.

We are living through extraordinary times, evidenced by growing chaos, wars, climate change, and an ecological abyss. We have forgotten our great earthly Mother, who gave humanity its birth and continually sustains and nourishes our existence and all other living and non-living forms. We have no other home, no other mother, only this fragile planet. Our very existence is being called into question as never before—that is, unless we change direction—which is my hope.

In the book Spiritual Ecology, Llewellyn Vaughan-Lee writes, "The world is not a problem to be solved; it is a living being to which we belong. The world is part of our own self, and we are a part of its suffering wholeness. Until we go to the root of our image of separateness, there can

1. Willigis Jäger *Search for the Meaning of Life: Essays and Reflections* on the Mystical Experience (Liguori, MO: Triumph Books, 1995), 212.

be no healing. And the deepest part of our separateness from creation lies in our forgetfulness of its sacred nature, which is also our own sacred nature."[2]

As the great Chief Seattle of the Duwamish people, here on the West Coast, said so long ago: "What befalls the earth befalls all the sons and daughters of the earth. This we know—the earth does not belong to us; we belong to the earth. All things are connected like the blood that unites us all. Humankind does not weave the web of life; we are merely a strand in it. Whatever we do to the web, we do to ourselves."[3]

Spirituality teaches us that only love, empathy, and generosity allow us to live together to the full potential of human existence. In Zen and the mystical paths, awakening and spiritual life are not isolating adventures, for they inevitably lead us to fully participate in life in a new manner. We realize that we cannot stay forever in the stillness of our inner lives, for we are called to share the experience of love and belonging with others and contribute to the welfare of all things. This becomes imperative when we realize our utter interdependence with life on this astonishing planet and in this unimaginable universe. This wisdom is the foundation of all the great world's spiritual and mystical teachings.

I hope that you, my dear reader, will be touched by the mystic impulse that leads to the ground of your being. When you walk this path, may your journey be fruitful, and may you share what you find with others for the benefit of all.

2. Llewellyn Vaughan-Lee, editor *Spiritual Ecology: The Cry of the Earth* (2016 Point Reyes, CA: The Golden Sufi Center, 2016), v.

3. Chief Seattle based on the original statement given December 1854. See Internet source: https://www.csun.edu/~vcpsy00h/seattle.htm

Appendix 1

A Short Biography of Willigis Jäger

Willigis Jäger, OSB (1925-2020) was a German Benedictine monk, mystic, and Zen master. He was one of Europe's most important contemporary pioneers of trans-confessional spirituality. As a Zen and Christian contemplative teacher, Willigis inspired and accompanied thousands of people of various faiths. His life and work personified a deep yearning for religious and mystical experience and understanding, which he vigorously pursued with great conviction, courage, and energy. Willigis's lifework was to promote a contemporary vision and interpretation of the unity of the mystical experience, especially in the Christian contemplative and Zen Buddhist traditions. The following is an outline of his life, the development of his work, and its significant influences and insights.

Willigis was born in the German town of Hösbach. His early youth was carefree and happy. He was raised in a devout Catholic home by working-class parents and six siblings. An active child, he soon acquired a lifelong love of the outdoors and sporting activities. His disposition was reflected in his nickname, *Frech und Fromm,* which means cheeky and pious.

When Willigis was still young, one particular experience strongly shaped his lifelong interest in spirituality. He wrote that when he was six, he experienced a transcendent moment for the first time. This occurred when Willigis was not yet in school, and his mother took him to church, which was nearly empty except for the burning candles on the altar and the scent of incense wafting through the air. It was the Eucharistic devotion of Perpetual Adoration, with the Sanctuary exposed and a few solemn elderly folks chanting the rosary at the back of the church. Their monotonous voices and the church atmosphere lifted him out of his ordinary consciousness, making everything appear in a different light—yet more real, yet strangely detached from everyday reality. He didn't know what was happening to him, but it gave him certainty that absolute love was waiting behind everything.[1]

As a youth, Willigis attended a Benedictine boarding school until the Nazi authorities closed it down during the war. Despite his negative view of Hitler and National Socialism, he was unwillingly conscripted into military service near the end of the Second World War. Still, unlike many friends and family members, he survived the ordeal of those difficult times.

Undoubtedly, Willigis's early life experiences, schooling, and the disastrous war years all contributed to his desire to pursue a religious and spiritual life. So Willigis joined the Benedictine community in 1945; two years later, in 1947, Willigis entered the Benedictine abbey in Münsterschwarzach in northern Bavaria and began his monastic formation, which included studying philosophy and theology. In 1952, he was ordained a priest and worked for seven years as a prefect and teacher at the boarding school and high school at Münsterschwarzach Abbey. In 1960, he became a consultant for mission and development at the Association of German Catholic Youth and, in the same year, co-founded the ecumenical outreach Action Missio, which took him to many countries, including Asia and Japan.

Throughout Willigis's monastic formation and early years as a monk and priest, he maintained an abiding interest in Christian mystical writing and practice, which was not necessarily encouraged by his superiors. Still, he persisted in his contemplative practices and studies of the past mystical teachings in the Catholic church, such as Meister Eckhart, John of the Cross, Teressa of Ávila, etc.[2]

1. Willigis Jäger *Über Die Liebe* (München: Kösel-Verlag, 2011), 123. & *Das Leben ist Religion* (Berlin: Kösel-Verlag, 2007), 20. & Richard McDaniel *Catholicism and Zen* (Nepean, ON: Sumeru Press, 2016) Kindle 89.

2. Willigis Jäger *Über Die Liebe* (München: Kösel-Verlag, 2011) & Willigis Jäger im Gespräch mit Paul J. Kohtes *Ein Leben Für Das Wesentliche* (Bielefeld: Theseus in Kamphausen Verlag Media, 2010) DVD.

In the early 1970s, Willigis was introduced to Zen by Father Hugo Enomiya Lasalle (1898-1990), a famous Jesuit priest who had lived in Hiroshima, Japan, since the late 1920s (and who had survived the mass destruction of the American atomic bomb attack in 1945)[3]. Lasalle was one of the first Westerners to train in Zen, starting in the early 1930s; he was influential in drawing many Catholics and Christians to the reformed Zen movement known then as Sanbo Kyodan (also referred to as the Harada-Yasutani lineage named after its first two Zen masters, Daiun Sogaku Harada and Hakuun Yasutani). Fr. Lassalle studied with these Zen masters until their deaths and continued with their lineage successor, Yamada Koun Roshi (1907-1989).

Willigis wrote that he attended his first Zen seminar with Father E. Lassalle at his home monastery in Münsterschwarzach. He immediately recognized Zen as the path he needed to follow, believing it would lead him to a deeper spiritual understanding. He began practicing regularly and quickly felt reassured that he was on the right track. Two retreats followed with Brigitte D'Ortschy Roshi, during which he realized that only great perseverance and unwavering commitment would enable him to progress further in his practice. In time, an opportunity arose to study Zen in depth when his community allowed him to join a newly established mission in Japan, which he viewed as a divine opportunity. Thus, at the peak of his professional commitments, he decided to leave his position at Action Missio, despite the disapproval of some friends, to join a newly founded Catholic mission house in Kamakura and practice Zen with Yamada Koun Roshi, whom he had previously met in Munich during 1971. Remarkably, his new community was in the same city where Yamada Koun Roshi had his center.[4]

Thus, in 1975, after receiving permission from his Benedictine superiors and moving to Kamakura, Japan, Willigis began an intensive six-year Zen training under Yamada Roshi, the head of the Sanbo Kyodan

3. John Hersey *Hiroshima* (New York: Alfred Knopf, 1946), 56-65. & Richard McDaniel *Catholicism and Zen* (Nepean, ON: Sumeru Press, 2016) Kindle 37.

4. Willigis Jäger *Über Die Liebe* (München: Kösel-Verlag, 2011), 128-129. & Richard McDaniel *Catholicism and Zen* (Nepean, ON: Sumeru Press, 2016) Kindle 89.

lineage of Zen Buddhism. Sanbo Kyodan is primarily a secular lineage that deemphasized the separation between laypeople and the ordained, and it mixed the teachings and practices of the two predominant Zen traditions in Japan (i.e., the Soto and Rinzai lineages). Most importantly, Yamada Roshi was among the few Japanese Zen masters who accepted non-Buddhists as students, most of whom were devoted Christians. Initially, Willigis saw Zen as a way to deepen and supplement his Christian practice and understanding of mysticism, a view that inevitably changed the longer he practiced and grew in his understanding.

According to the Jesuit Fr. Ruben Habito, Yamada believed that given the proper guidance, a person assiduous in practice could lead to a pure and genuine Zen experience, whether that person was a professed Buddhist, Christian, or some other belief. Yamada stressed that Zen practice makes the Buddhist more fully a Buddhist and suggested that the Christian could be a better Christian by practicing and living a Zen life.[5]

It is worth mentioning that the Sanbo Kyodan lineage of Zen Buddhism has significantly impacted the establishment and practice of Zen in the West. Several pioneering Zen teachers in North America, such as Philip Kapleau Roshi, Taizan Maezumi Roshi, and Robert Aitken Roshi, came from this tradition, and their lineages continue to thrive today.

Willigis's experiences and extended stay in Kamakura helped him recognize the essential unity of mystical experience, especially in the context of the Zen Buddhist and Christian traditions, despite their outward differences. His time in Japan was marked by intensive training, sitting for many hours daily in Yamada Roshi's meditation hall, going to regular private interviews, attending his formal talks and retreat intensives, doing formal *koan* study, working in the garden, and getting to know his teacher on a personal basis. During the six years, he also spent six months in a hermitage to deepen his practice and experience.

5. Ruben Habito *In Memoriam: Yamada Kōun Rōshi* article in Buddhist-Christian Studies Journal (Honolulu: University of Hawaii Press, 1990), 236.

By all accounts, Willigis had some profound experiences during his Zen training in Japan, including what Zen calls *kensho* or awakening experiences (literally, seeing one's true nature). He recognized the similarity of his kensho experience to what he already knew from his practice and understanding of Christian mysticism. In one of his writings, he described practicing with *Mu* (a word koan used in meditation) for three years, which felt much like his earlier meditative practice with the word *Gott* (God). Having an experienced teacher helped him navigate challenges and allowed his previous deep insights (in contemplation) to return. With each *Sesshin* (intensive meditation retreat), he sensed progress. He likened the kensho experience to the gradual unfolding of a flower, culminating in a powerful awakening one night after a session, when he felt as if the flower's last petals burst open with great intensity. At that moment, he experienced only emptiness, which he likened to the 'nada, nada, nada.' of St. John of the Cross. In this emptiness, there was only the present moment, the awareness of the breath, and, upon rising, just the pure act of moving. His teacher, Yamada Roshi, later acknowledged this as a kensho moment. When reflecting on his experience, he identified several key themes: love, emptiness, fullness, unity, and happiness.[6]

Additionally, he described this kensho experience as lacking any dramatic conclusion; it felt more like an invitation to a deeper, more joyful reality—marked by overwhelming silence and emptiness. Sitting in wonder, he remained in this altered state for a full day. All sense of division disappeared, and everything existed as it truly was. When a crow cawed outside, it simply was—nothing more. The reality created by his intellect faded away, leaving no images in the stillness and silence, while any attempt to express this experience in words proved inadequate.[7]

During the six years in Japan, Willigis compared and integrated what he was learning in Zen with his Christian understanding, one that gave new meaning to his interpretation of Christ and the Apostles' teaching in the Gospels, as well as the Christian mystics, such as Meister Eckhart,

6. Willigis Jäger *Über Die Liebe* (München: Kösel-Verlag, 2011), 129.
7. Willigis Jäger *Das Leben ist Religion* (Berlin: Kösel-Verlag, 2007), 72.

John of the Cross and Teresa of Ávila. Willigis wrote his first book about Christian Contemplation during this time.[8]

From his experience in Zen, Willigis recognized four fundamental aspects that contributed to how he would later see and teach Zen and Contemplation. His viewpoint and interpretation of Zen and mysticism were considered radical by many Christians and some Zen practitioners, both then and still now.

First, he understood that Zen meditation profoundly transforms one's religious beliefs. Second, he believed the practice must adapt to the Western zeitgeist to flourish. Third, he was convinced that authentic mystical experiences have a fundamental unity, no matter their culture or spirituality. Fourth, the Zen experience was neither a religion nor bound to one; although it came from Buddhism, it was not limited by religious doctrine.

Willigis believed that Zen would inevitably change in its outward form in the West, just as it did when encountering Taoist China. Still, its fundamental essence could not be distorted by either Christians or Buddhists—in his words, *the Dharma needed no defenders.* From his extended stay in Japan, he saw that the religious ideas of his Buddhist friends changed just as much when they practiced Zazen (Zen meditation) as the religious ideas of his Christian friends.[9]

Willigis became increasingly convinced that Zen is not fundamentally a religion. He believed it was unfortunate that many Zen teachers in the East and the West were too closely tied to their religious affiliations. Willigis argued that the insights of awakening from Zen practice encourage us to rise above our religious identities. He maintained that the core differences among religions are not vertical between denominations but horizontal between their esoteric and exoteric levels. Every religion has an exoteric, or outward, aspect that includes creeds, holy scriptures, rituals, and ceremonies, which most followers engage with. However, all

8. Willigis Jäger *Das Leben ist Religion* (Berlin: Kösel-Verlag, 2007), 77-81.
9. Willigis Jäger *Das Leben ist Religion* (Berlin: Kösel-Verlag, 2007), 94.

religions also provide a spiritual path that transcends specific doctrines—an esoteric path that leads to experiences that their teachings can only attempt to describe.[10]

In 1980, Yamada Roshi gave Willigis authority to teach Zen. The following year, he returned to Germany to his Münsterschwarzach Abbey, where he resumed his pastoral duties as a Benedictine priest and monk and started to advocate and teach the practice of contemplation and Zen throughout Germany and Europe. He instructed Catholics, lay and ordained alike, those of other Christian faiths, and anyone interested. Willigis was a natural promoter and reformer; he wanted to bring what he discovered in the Zen experience to the Catholic and greater Christian community. He hoped for a renewal of the tradition of contemplative spirituality in the churches. This attitude was in line with the reforming spirit of Vatican II, which put him at odds with the resurgent conservative tendencies within the Catholic Church.

In 1983, he founded his first Zen and Contemplation center, the Haus St. Benedikt, in the former Würzburg boarding school of Münsterschwarzach Abbey. His teacher, Yamada Roshi, traveled to Germany to inaugurate the newly founded Würzburg center.

During the 1980s, Willigis also traveled to North America to hold yearly retreats at Our Lady of Guadalupe Trappist Abbey near Portland, Oregon, where he inspired the Abbot to build a meditation hall next to the cloistered monastery.[11] He also returned yearly to Kamakura, Japan, to study under Yamada Roshi until 1989 (when Yamada died).

During this decade, Willigis focused on providing spiritual direction to his students. He aimed to help them avoid the pitfalls he had encountered in Zen, contemplative practices, and spiritual training. Drawing inspiration from the personal guidance he received from Yamada Roshi, Willigis realized that instead of steering seekers toward more conventional

10. Willigis Jäger *Das Leben ist Religion* (Berlin: Kösel-Verlag, 2007), 93.

11. Seven Thunders organization website, Portland, Oregon. Internet source https://seventhunders.org/about/ & Richard McDaniel *Catholicism and Zen* (Nepean, ON: Sumeru Press, 2016) Kindle 169-172.

practices, such as prayer, during challenging times, he should encourage them to stick with their Zen and contemplative practices—even when they faced dryness, loneliness, and despondency; which he saw as part of the purification process. He believed that enduring such difficulties would lead to lasting spiritual growth and awakening for his students. Willigis's approach to supporting his students along their spiritual journeys in the various Zen and contemplation courses at the St. Benedikt house was by all accounts a great success and attracted many students.[12]

In 1990, Willigis helped found, together with Protestant and Catholic priests and religious teachers, the Ecumenical Working Group on Contemplative Prayer, from which the Würzburg School of Contemplation later emerged. The school aimed to revive contemplative prayer and mysticism in Christian churches.

In 1996, Kubota Roshi, Yamada Kuon's successor as head of the Sanbo Kyodan lineage, presented Willigis with full Dharma transmission and formally recognized him as a Zen Master (a Rōshi in the Japanese Zen tradition). Thus, his formal teaching name and title were Koun Rōshi. The word Koun (or sometimes spelled Kyo-un) means *empty cloud,* which later became the name of his lineage, *Leere Wolke,* in German.

Willigis's popularity as a teacher and spiritual director steadily increased during the 1980s and 1990s, attracting a diverse audience of followers and supporters both within and outside the Christian community. Willigis wrote that he began to notice a shift in the people seeking his guidance; no longer just those religiously educated came to him. An increasing number of individuals who did not identify with any religion or had distanced themselves from their churches began to seek him out for spiritual direction. Many felt disconnected, believing that their religion of birth no longer resonated with their contemporary life. Consequently, many had turned to alternative spiritual practices, including the Eastern traditions and Sufism. Following the significant

12. Willigis Jäger *Das Leben ist Religion* (Berlin: Kösel-Verlag, 2007), 112. & *Jetzr Nichts Sein - Ein Inspirationbuch zum 90 Geburtstag von Willigis Jäger*, a compilation of various contributors edited by Christoph Quarch (Holzkirchen: West-Östliche Weisheit Willigis Jäger Stiftung, 2015).

political changes and move towards reunification of Germany in 1989, an increasing number of people from the former communist East Germany—who had no previous religious formation or background—also started attending. Willigis and his House of St. Benedict offered these seekers a path that embraced the fundamental principles of mysticism from both Eastern and Western traditions without requiring any confession of faith.[13]

As Willigis's fame grew, he wrote books on Christian Contemplation and Zen, and he became more frequently interviewed and published in journals and magazines, both religious and secular. Willigis also encouraged others to teach and to start groups in their hometowns. By all accounts, Willigis was much admired and beloved by his students within his Catholic Church and beyond.[14]

By 2000, his writings, especially *Die Welle ist das Meer* (English edition: *Mysticism for Modern Times*)[15], brought success, difficulties, and unforeseen changes to Willigis Jäger's life. This book was a German national bestseller but attracted the attention of the church and religious leaders. A conservative Catholic group from his home diocese of Würzburg complained about Willigis to Rome's Congregation for the Doctrine of the Faith, under its then leader - Cardinal Josef Ratzinger (who went on to reign as Pope Benedict XVI from 2005 to 2013). As a result, Willigis's works were meticulously examined, and several theological statements were found objectionable to Catholic orthodoxy.

In 2002, the Congregation for the Doctrine of the Faith demanded a retraction of the objectionable statements. It issued him a ban on speaking and writing, which Willigis refused to comply with. However, Willigis soon negotiated, by mutual agreement, a leave of absence (exclusion)

13. Willigis Jäger *Das Leben ist Religion* (Berlin: Kösel-Verlag, 2007), 121-122.

14. *Jetzr Nichts Sein - Ein Inspirationbuch zum 90 Geburtstag von Willigis Jäger*, a compilation of various contributors edited by Christoph Quarch (Holzkirchen: West-Östliche Weisheit Willigis Jäger Stiftung, 2015).

15. Christoph Quarch *Die Heilsame Leere* (article in Horizonte Fliege Zeitschrift, 2008) Internet Source https://west-oestliche-weisheit.de/ueber-uns/veroeffentlichungen-willigis-jaeger/artikel-von-und-ueber-willigis-jaeger/

from his Benedictine monastery. This meant that Willigis did not have to renounce his monastic vows, return to lay status, or lose his membership in the Catholic church. However, Willigis did have to separate his teaching activity from the abbey. Otherwise, he remained attached to his Benedictine community.

Nevertheless, Willigis was admired and beloved by many within the Catholic Church despite facing significant challenges from Vatican authorities who criticized him. These difficulties often placed Willigis, like many mystics, at odds with the formal structures of the Church that he valued. By this time, many of Willigis's beliefs diverged from Catholic orthodoxy. For example, he did not believe in the *physical* resurrection of Christ after his death or in his ascension into heaven; for Willigis, these were symbolic stories that held spiritual significance rather than literal truths. He also believed that God was not separate from creation and that the existing inequality of women in the Church was unacceptable, amongst other opinions.

Willigis was seventy-seven years old and firmly committed to his monastic vocation, spiritual understanding, and life's vision when he suddenly found himself in a new, unforeseen situation without a place to live, work, or teach. However, by the following year, Willigis relocated his living and teaching activities to a new facility.

In early 2003, thanks to the support and patronage of Willigis's longtime spiritual companions (Gertraud Gruber, a wealthy entrepreneur, and the couple Irene and Gerhard Bopp), a former monastery in Holzkirchen near Würzburg was purchased and rebuilt. This had been the site of an old Benedictine monastery in the past and, more recently, a hotel that had fallen into disuse and needed restoration. Its monastic foundations date back to the eighth century. The initial round of renovation was completed quickly, and the first programs started later that year, which allowed his courses to begin there in late 2003. The new center, Benediktushof, thus became Willigis Jäger's residence, teaching center, and ongoing project, reflecting his spiritual vision of an inter-religious meditation and mindfulness center.

Willigis continued writing, teaching, and guiding individuals during the next dozen years, with many of his most important books being published, such as (*Ewige Weisheit* (Eternal Wisdom), *Zen im 21. Jahrhundert* (Zen in the 21st Century), Über *Die Liebe* (About Love), and his biography *Das Leben is Religion* (Life is Religion), to name but a few. These books reflected his deepening understanding of spirituality and mystical practices and were more personal in tone, for example, of his near-death experience, which brought an absolute conviction that love underlies all existence.[16]

In his talks and published works, he started using the expression integral spirituality, followed later by trans-confessional spirituality. This phrase expressed his conviction that the mystical experience and path were universal and transpersonal, that they flowed from eternal wisdom and were open to anyone regardless of belief or creed. Therefore, in this sense, Willigis's use of the word confession meant one's religious affiliation or spiritual beliefs, including agnostic and atheistic perspectives, such as those in science.

During this decade, Willigis increasingly talked about the transcendent nature of mystical experiences and the inspiration and understanding he gained from a lifetime devoted to studying and following the paths of Christ and the Buddha—two spiritual traditions that guided him toward his awakening. Willigis asserted that a deep kensho experience, or mystical enlightenment, goes beyond the confines of any religion—just as Buddha Nature or Christ Consciousness transcends the personhood of Siddhartha Gautama and Jesus. He often reiterated that Zen transcends Buddhism just as Christian mysticism transcends its denominational boundaries. For Willigis, the essence of both traditions lies on a transrational, mystical level. He emphasized that for those who have arrived at this level, the experience is often so profound that it compels them to reevaluate their religious understanding.[17]

16. Willigis Jäger *Über Die Liebe* (München: Kösel-Verlag, 2011), 132-133.

17. Willigis Jäger *Christus und Buddha* - Artikel (Holzkirchen, DE: West-Östliche Eisheit Willigis Jäger Stiftung). Internet source https://west-oestliche-weisheit.de/ueber-uns/veroeffentlichungen-willigis-jaeger)

In 2007, Willigis, with the support of Professor Hans Wielens, founded the *West-Östliche Weisheit Willigis Jäger Stiftung* (West-Eastern Wisdom Willigis Jäger Foundation), which is based at Benediktushof. The foundation's mandate is to aid the ongoing development of Willigis's work and legacy in Zen and Christian Contemplation. It is also committed to researching, designing, and promoting contemporary spirituality.

In June 2009, Willigis formally left the Sambo Kyodan lineage to start his independent lineage, the Zen line *Leere Wolke* (Empty Cloud), one that was in accord with his trans-confessional vision and the reframing of Zen for Europe and the West. The lineage's teachers and school remained centered at Benediktushof, where Willigis lived.

Later that same year, he received Dharma confirmation as a Chan (Zen) master from Master Jing Hui, Abbot of the Bailin Temple in Hebei Province, China. During the ceremony, there was a minor incident that reflects Willigis's endeavor to break free from the traditional features of the rituals of Asian Zen. His longtime student and colleague Alexander Poraj wrote that it would have been customary for Willigis to wear the monkish Chan robe during the ceremony. But Willigis refused to do so, and as he explained to his companions afterward, the Chinese way of institutionalizing Chan was far too similar to his Catholic Church. He wanted to avoid regressing in that direction at all costs, even for the sake of Zen."[18]

In his teaching career, Willigis never wore traditional Zen garbs and usually didn't wear Benedictine robes. But he would don his priestly vestments when appropriate on such occasions as baptisms, funerals, marriage blessings, etc. Also, he preferred to be called Willigis by those he accompanied, and he thought of his community as a fellowship of companions on the spiritual path. Willigis embodied a humble Benedictine attitude that espoused compassion, equality, and respect for one and all; in other words, he avoided grandiosity in his speaking and

18. Alexander Poraj-Zakiej *Das Willigis Jahrhundert* (Holzkirchen: West-Östliche Weisheit Willigis Jäger Stiftung 2020), 187.

lifestyle. These qualities were deeply admired by his students, friends, and supporters.

In 2010, Willigis Jäger and other longtime Christian companions founded the Contemplation line *Wolke des Nichtwissens* (Cloud of Unknowing). In doing so, Willigis assured his legacy by establishing two lines based at Benediktushof: a Christian Contemplation path and a trans-confessional Zen path. Both lines remain independent within the general direction of his foundation.

In setting up these two lines, Willigis also named his designated successors and tasked them with continuing the work of the Zen and Contemplation teaching lines. In the Zen line, this meant incorporating and adapting the most suitable practices from both the Japanese and Chinese traditions into the Western environment. This process included a revisioning of certain characteristics within traditional Zen; in particular, the *Leere Wolke* (Empty Cloud) lineage believes in recognition of the equality of the sexes, that ordination is unnecessary to practice Zen (including becoming a teacher in the lineage), and that the path of Zen is open to all—regardless of one's convictions, beliefs or religion. Lastly, this Zen line aspires to an ongoing dialogue with the modern sciences.

The Wolke des Nichtwissens (Cloud of Unknowing) contemplative line focuses on making Christian mystical teachings and practices accessible to people in their contemporary lives. This means that those who practice contemplation are now mostly laypersons living in an ever-growing secular world, and thus, no longer mainly nuns or monks as they were in past ages. The line seeks to build a Christian fellowship centered on contemplative learning, practice, and community. In addition, its teachers strive to promote the practice of contemplation in their faith communities and affiliations, as well as offer courses and support for students. It also seeks interchange with the sciences.

In 2016, Willigis Jäger withdrew from his many years of teaching and spiritual accompaniment due to his age and declining health and memory, although he continued to reside at Benediktushof. In March

2020, Willigis died peacefully shortly after his 95th Birthday. Until the end, he was lovingly accompanied and cared for by people close to him at Benediktushof. According to his wish, his Benedictine brothers and sisters buried him at the cemetery of the Münsterschwarzach Abbey in a moving ceremony.

Appendix 2

The Author's Concise Biography

Arnie Lade is an internationally recognized acupuncturist, author, and teacher specializing in complementary and energetic healing. He has been in practice for five decades and lives in Victoria, BC, Canada.

Arnie is the author of numerous books, including *Energetic Healing: Embracing the Life Force*; *Acupuncture Points: Images and Functions*; coauthor of *Tao and Dharma: Chinese Medicine and Ayurveda*; and a contributing author of *Chinese Exercises and Massage*.

Arnie studied with Willigis Jäger, a Benedictine monk, priest, and Zen master. He is a Zen teacher in the Empty Cloud lineage (*Zen-Linie Leere Wolke*) based in Benediktushof, Germany.

Arnie has had a lifelong interest in spirituality. He grew up in a Catholic home and explored Buddhist, Taoist, and Hindu practices as an adult. He has also studied ways to help himself, such as the Feldenkrais Method, and generally meanders through life, making a mess (one mistake after another) in the search for meaning and wholeness.

ENDORSEMENTS FOR
Zen *and the* Mystic Impulse

"Part personal reflection and part homage to the Catholic Benedictine monk and Zen Master, Willigis Jäger, but primarily a clearly written introduction to what Jäger called the Sophia Perennis, the universal spiritual connection underlying all religious traditions. Deserving of a slow, reflective reading."

— *Richard Bryan McDaniel,*
author of *Catholicism and Zen* and *The Story of Zen*

"Intimacy is the essence of Zen. Arnie Lade's profound offering carries a deeply intimate portrayal of his teacher, Willigis Jäger. Reading this book gave me the feeling of being in the presence of a humble, wise friend. This transmission from Willigis through Arnie is a great gift for anyone on any spiritual path."

— *Russell Delman*
Founder of the Embodied Life School

"When the world seems to fall apart, it's even more important to be well-rooted. Zen and mystical practices have the ability to access the deeper layers of human existence and to both energize and calm our souls. This, however, requires experienced guidance as provided by Arnie Lade through his insights and reflections on the teachings of Willigis Jäger, a modern-day Christian mystic and Zen Master."

— *Dr. Christoph Quarch*
Philosopher and author

More Titles *from* Arnie Lade

Energetic Healing: Embracing the Life Force
Arnie Lade • ISBN: 9780914955467 • $17.95 • 280 pgs.

Energetic Healing: Embracing the Life Force is a guide to the inner landscape of the subtle energy. In this groundbreaking book the role of manifestation, utility and healing power of our life force/energy is explored in a concise and informative fashion. Furthermore, a compelling and original model of energy is provided, one that bridges many seemingly separate disciplines to reveal their unity and usefulness. Discover for yourself the unique expressions of energy that bind body, mind and spirit together.

Tao and Dharma: Chinese Medicine and Ayurveda
Robert Svoboda & Arnie Lade • ISBN: 9780914955214
$12.95 • 155 pgs.

Tao and Dharma: Chinese Medicine and Ayurveda explores the enduring features of humanity's longest and continually practiced systems of medicine. These two indigenous healing arts arising independently in China and India communed and exchanged experience, techniques, and therapeutic substances over hte epochs of their development. This book's interesting and valuable comparison provides a pioneer effort in examining side-by-side two great systmes of medicine, studying closely the historical, theoretical and practical relationships. In so doing it offers these ancient paradigms into the practice of modern healing for a synergistic, inclusive approach.